Spatial Reasoning PUZZLES

THAT MAKE KIDS THINK!

Grades 6–8

Spatial Reasoning PUZZLES

THAT MAKE KIDS THINK!

JEFFREY J. WANKO

PRUFROCK PRESS INC.
WACO, TEXAS

Prufrock Press Inc.
P.O. Box 8813
Waco, TX 76714-8813
Phone: (800) 998-2208
Fax: (800) 240-0333
http://www.prufrock.com

Table of Contents

Introduction—1

Chapter 1: Slitherlink—5

Chapter 2: Hashiwokakero—29

Chapter 3: Masyu—55

Chapter 4: Yajilin—79

Blank Grids to Create Your
Own Puzzles—109

Solutions—125

References—145

About the Author—147

Introduction

In the last few decades, hundreds of different types of logic puzzles have been introduced. Many of these puzzles have originated in Japan, where puzzle magazines like *Nikoli* have strived to create new and challenging puzzles for solvers. *Nikoli* popularized Sudoku puzzles and helped make them a worldwide phenomenon—along with computer programs that were written to generate Sudoku puzzles for newspapers, magazines, and puzzle books.

Sudoku puzzles (and their variations) are great tools for learning deductive reasoning skills—the step-by-step logic that is used in many mathematical and other situations. But deductive reasoning is not the only type of logic that can be learned.

In this book, you will learn more about the development of *spatial reasoning* through the use of a few of the other types of logic puzzles that exist—in particular, a subcategory of puzzles known as *path puzzles*. In path puzzles, the solver is challenged to create a path that follows some specific rules that govern the placement of the path. The solver would need to use deductive reasoning to place the path while also employing spatial reasoning to get an overall view of what the path would look like.

For example, one type of puzzle might be presented in a square grid with some of the boxes already shaded in (see Figure 0.1). In this puzzle, the solver is asked to place a closed loop path (a path that connects back to itself and doesn't cross itself) that runs through the middle of all of the unshaded boxes in the grid and that travels only in horizontal and vertical segments (see Figure 0.2). As with all logic puzzles, the solution is unique.

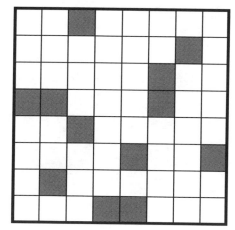

Figure 0.1. Example path puzzle.

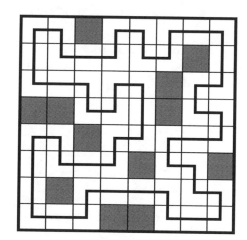

Figure 0.2. Example path puzzle solution.

The solution path can be found using deductive reasoning, but with path puzzles, it can also be helpful to employ some spatial reasoning when working on a solution. In this example, a solver might start by looking at one region (like the bottom left corner) of the puzzle grid and envisioning how the path might work its way through the white squares. Boxes that have only two open sides (sides not blocked by an edge of the grid or a shaded box) are easy places to start drawing pieces of the path, but taking a step back and looking at a region or the puzzle overall can give a solver a relatively clear sense of how to fill in a solution.

Some argue that spatial reasoning is innate—that someone is either born with it or not. Others contend that males are better at spatial reasoning tasks than females. Neither one of these statements is entirely accurate.

Research has shown that while some people may start out better with spatial tasks, this type of reasoning can be improved dramatically through the application of spatial visualization tasks (Ben-Chaim, Lappan, & Houang, 1988). And although males tend to outperform females on some spatial reasoning tasks, there is no evidence of gender differences in logical reasoning ability (Battista, 1990).

Using This Book

In this book, four different types of logic path puzzles are presented—Slitherlink, Hashiwokakero, Masyu, and Yajilin. Each type of puzzle is very different from the others, yet they all involve creating paths.

One of the best ways to introduce a new puzzle type to students is to show them a few unsolved puzzle grids along with their accompanying solutions—but no rules for solving and no description of the goal for each type of puzzle. Students are then asked to make some observations about the puzzles and their solutions and to come up with a list of what they think the goal and the rules are for that type of puzzle. This forces students to look carefully at the examples and to draw conclusions about what they see. Students are already using their critical thinking skills before they start solving the puzzles! (You'll find ready-to-use worksheets to do this activity at the end of each chapter.)

For example, the puzzles shown on page 3 are known as Suraromu—another type of path puzzle created by *Nikoli*. For each of the two puzzles, you are given the starting grid and the solution grid. Can you deduce the goal and the rules for Suraromu from these two examples?

Figure 0.3. Suraromu Puzzle 1.

Figure 0.4. Suraromu Puzzle 1 solution.

Figure 0.5. Suraromu Puzzle 2.

Figure 0.6. Suraromu Puzzle 2 solution.

The first observation that you might make is that this is another closed loop puzzle—that is, the goal of the puzzle is to create a path that joins back upon itself without crossing its path. (Three of the four types of puzzles in this book are also closed loop puzzles.) In Suraromu, the loop appears to stop and start at the circled number in the grid.

Another observation that is also made is that there are boxes with dotted lines in them and that the path travels through all of the these boxes (in Puzzle 1) or most of these boxes (in Puzzle 2). In fact, the dotted lines hold the key to figuring out Suraromu puzzles.

It might help to know that in the United States, Suraromu puzzles have been published under the name Slalom puzzles. In a slalom course, skiers race through numbered gates to the finish line. The path that you must draw in a Suraromu puzzle is like the route in a slalom course—you must travel through the numbered gates from the start to the finish.

In Puzzle 1, you may have noticed that the circled number in the grid (the 5) is the same as the total number of boxes with dotted lines in the them. These dotted lines are like the gates in a slalom ski course. In Puzzle 2, there are some boxes with dotted lines that are not used in the solution path (two of the boxes to the left of the number 8). Why are these two puzzles different in this respect?

If you consider the three boxes to the left of the 8 in Puzzle 2 as one gate (they are, after all, connected in one straight line), then Puzzle 2 really is no different from Puzzle 1. In each example, the solution path travels through each gate once and the total number of gates in the puzzle is the same as the circled number in the grid. Two examples may not be enough to show that this is the case with every Suraromu puzzle, but this looks to be true from these two samples.

But what about the path itself? Because there is exactly one solution to each puzzle, there must be some other rules that govern the placement of the solution path. Thinking back to skiing, the slalom course runs through *numbered* gates—this is also true in a Suraromu puzzle. The numbers that appear in some of the black squares indicate the number of the gate associated with those squares. Sometimes both sides of the gate are numbered (the 2s and the 4s in both examples) and sometimes only one side of the gate is numbered (the 1, 8, and 10 in Puzzle 2).

If you follow the solution path from the circled number, one of the directions will travel through gate 1 first, gate 2 second, and so on until it arrives back at the circled number. This rule is extremely important for finding the solution path, and it helps to govern the path so that there is exactly one solution.

Trying to figure out a puzzle's goal and rules is a great introductory activity to any new type of puzzle. Again, a worksheet with this activity has been provided for each of the four types of puzzles in this book.

Creating Puzzles

Each chapter in this book includes information about solving the puzzles and suggestions for creating puzzles. Blank grids are also provided for students to use when creating the puzzles. Students who have mastered solving the puzzles can be challenged to create more examples of the puzzles for others to solve. This is an excellent activity for students to do—especially to encourage them to apply their deductive and spatial reasoning skills to ensure that there is exactly one solution to each puzzle. Suggestions are also provided for extending this activity to include different themes for the puzzles and for developing new variations on the puzzle types. The sky is the limit!

Chapter 1

Slitherlink

The first path puzzle is commonly known as Slitherlink, although it can be found under many other names like Fences and Loop the Loop. It was introduced by the Japanese puzzle magazine *Nikoli* in 1989 and has since produced many different variations.

A standard Slitherlink puzzle consists of a square array of dots with numbers placed in some of the open spaces (see Figure 1.1). The goal of a Slitherlink puzzle is to create a single closed loop by connecting the dots using horizontal and vertical line segments. The numbers in the grid indicate the number of line segments around the number that are part of the closed loop (see Figure 1.2). Spaces without numbers could be surrounded by 0, 1, 2, or 3 line segments in the solution—the solver has to determine the entire path without knowing the number of segments surrounding the blank spaces. Using logic and spatial reasoning, a solver can deduce the unique solution to each Slitherlink puzzle.

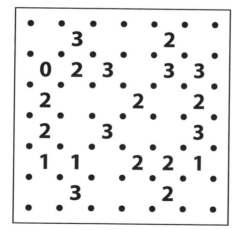

Figure 1.1. Example Slitherlink puzzle.

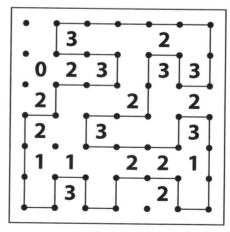

Figure 1.2. Example Slitherlink solution.

Solving the Example Puzzle

The key to solving a Slitherlink puzzle is to use spatial visualization to determine which segments need to be used to create the closed loop. With practice, a number of shortcuts can be found when numbers appear in certain patterns. A few of these shortcuts will be used in this discussion.

Starting with the combination of 0–2, both on the left edge of the puzzle, only two of the four sides around the two can be used to create the loop—the bottom and right sides. The side above the 2 cannot be used because the zero indicates that none of those surrounding sides are used. The left side of the 2 cannot be part of the loop because the path could not continue once it reaches the 0. This leaves the two sides shown in Figure 1.3. Also in Figure 1.3, the pieces of the grid that cannot be part of the solution are now marked with a small x. Some solvers find this notation helpful for eliminating some possibilities.

Each end of the path can also be continued as shown in Figure 1.4, because there is only one direction remaining in each case. The top left corner of the grid can also be filled with several more x's, since these spaces would lead to a dead-end in the path (see Figure 1.4).

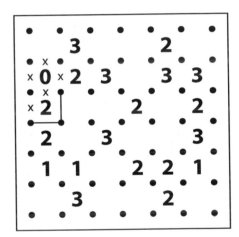

Figure 1.3. 0–2 combination on the edge.

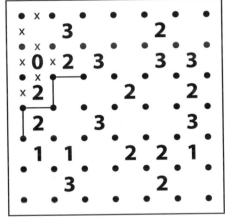

Figure 1.4. Additional x's and path pieces.

The 3 in the top row now presents an interesting situation. Three of the surrounding sides must be part of the loop and only one combination of three sides results in a part of the path that does not dead-end (Figure 1.5). Additionally, the 2 at the left of the fourth row already has two sides included in the path. When the other two sides are marked with x's, it becomes clear that the path continues down the left side of the grid (see Figure 1.5).

The 2 in the second row now has two of its surrounding sides included in the path. When its right side is marked with an x, the 3 to its right only has three possible sides remaining. The path at the top then continues two more spaces (see Figure 1.6). On the left side of the grid, additional x's are placed where the numbers are already satisfied and the path is forced to continue down and across the bottom edge of the grid (see Figure 1.6).

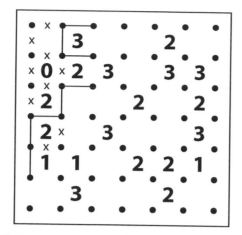

Figure 1.5. Surround the 3 in the top row.

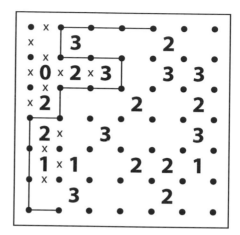

Figure 1.6. Surrounding another 3.

It is worth pointing out that the path is following one of the more popular shortcuts that can be found in Slitherlink puzzles—the path around diagonal 3s. When two 3s appear in the grid on a diagonal (as with the 3s that are now surrounded in the first and second rows), four different possibilities exist for the path (see Figure 1.7). In each case, the four outermost sides are always used. This information can be useful when solving a puzzle as these four sides can always be drawn when this situation occurs in a grid.

Another popular shortcut that can often be found in Slitherlink puzzles involves two 3s that appear adjacent to each other (as with the two 3s on the right side of the second row of the example puzzle). When this situation occurs, the path always snakes around the 3s in one of two ways (see Figure 1.8). In each case, the three parallel line segments are always used.

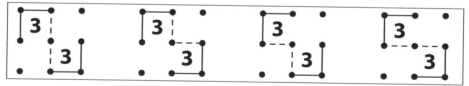

Figure 1.7. Diagonal 3s.

Figure 1.8. Adjacent 3s.

Returning to the example puzzle, only one of these two arrangements works with the 2 in the top row (see Figure 1.9)—the other one would only allow one side of the 2 in the top row to be used in the path. Likewise, only one arrangement works with the other end of the path to surround the 3 in the bottom row (see Figure 1.9).

The path already turns at one corner of the 2 near the middle of the grid. This means that of the four sides around this 2, both the top and left cannot be used for the path—so they can be marked with x's, leaving the bottom and right sides as part of the path (see Figure 1.10). From there, only one arrangement works to surround the 3 near the middle of the grid and join to one end of the existing path (see Figure 1.10).

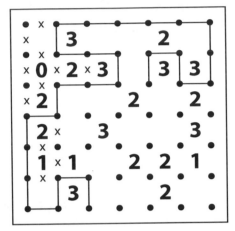

Figure 1.9. Snaking around the 3s.

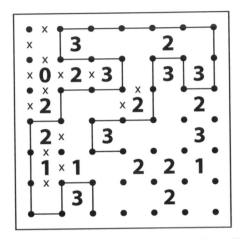

Figure 1.10. Surrounding another 3.

The unused 3 on the right side of the grid is now blocked in such a way that only one arrangement of segments allows the 3 to be surrounded (see Figure 1.11). The right side of the 1 below it must also be part of the path, so x's can be placed on the other two sides (see Figure 1.11). This step also shows that the path does not need to be found sequentially—sometimes the path develops in pieces and these pieces are combined to complete the entire closed loop.

Three of the four path ends can be extended only one way (see Figure 1.12).

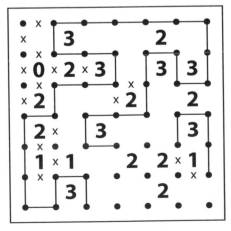

Figure 1.11. New part of the path.

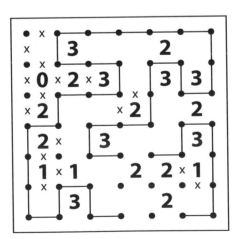

Figure 1.12. Extending some of the ends.

At this point, several different approaches can be taken to determine the final unique solution. In each case, the solver would consider each possibility for a specific part of the puzzle and determine which way(s) might lead to an incorrect solution. For example, the solver could focus on the 2 in the bottom row. There are two ways to continue the path from the bottom right corner around the 2—below the 2 and up on the left, or up on the right and above the 2 (see Figure 1.13).

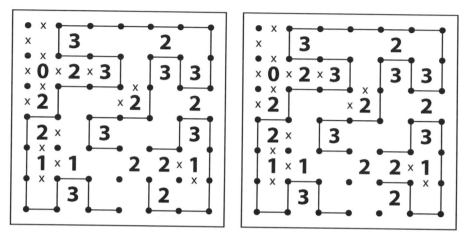

Figure 1.13. Two possible routes.

In each case, there is now only one way to satisfy the required number of sides for each number in the grid (see Figure 1.14). However, for the potential solution on the left, the path makes not one, but two closed loops. The unique correct solution is therefore on the right.

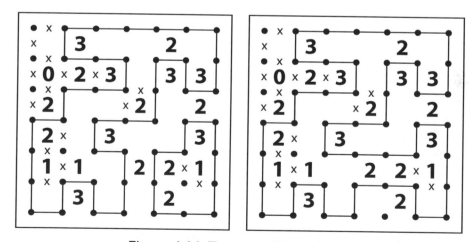

Figure 1.14. Two possible routes.

There are many other solving strategies that can be used when solving Slitherlink puzzles. New situations arise that require new analyses. Good Slitherlink puzzles allow the solver to explore new situations and to develop new approaches and short-cuts for solving Slitherlink puzzles.

Creating Slitherlink Puzzles

Slitherlink puzzles are relatively easy to create. One of the best ways to learn about solving this type of puzzle is to have one person create a path, fill in every number in the grid and remove the path, leaving only the numbers. A puzzle created this way has a unique solution but unlike the one used in this chapter as an example, there are no blank spaces. In fact, there are more clues than necessary to solve the puzzle. But the solver gets the experience of learning how different combinations of numbers work together in a puzzle to determine the path of the closed loop.

The challenge comes in removing some of the numbers—leaving enough so that the solution can still be determined using logic and spatial reasoning but not removing too many and creating a situation where more than one solution is possible. For example, the 3 x 3 Slitherlink in Figure 1.15 has four possible solutions. Each of the 2's in the top row allow the path to travel outside of the 2 or inside of it (see Figure 1.16).

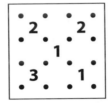

Figure 1.15. 3 x 3 Slitherlink.

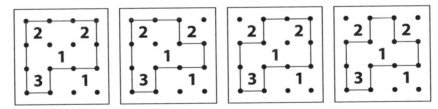

Figure 1.16. Four solutions.

A simple correction of adding numbers on the middle of both the left and right edge of the grid (see Figure 1.17) reduces the number of solutions to one. However, starting grids with more numbers are often easier to solve than ones with fewer numbers. It is up to the puzzle creator to determine how many numbers appear in the starting grid.

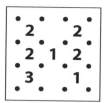

Figure 1.17. Corrected 3 x 3 Slitherlink.

The amount of starting numbers is not the only determination of a puzzle's difficulty level. Another critical factor is the relative placement of the numbers. Some creators of Slitherlink puzzles like to have patterns in the placement of their starting numbers. All of the puzzles in this book follow the practice of having 180° rotational symmetry in the placement of the numbers in the starting grids. This is typically done for aesthetics and as an extra challenge for the puzzle creator—it doesn't necessarily make the puzzle more or less difficult to solve. In fact, it usually means that there are numbers in a starting grid that are not necessary for solving the puzzle. But the puzzle creator may prefer to have them there to make the starting puzzle look better or more balanced.

The grouping of the numbers also determines the puzzle's difficulty level and the way that a solver may attack the puzzle. Puzzles with numbers that are grouped in ways that allow a solver to use some of the shortcuts that were alluded to earlier are a good way to start—they give a solver a direction as well as some insight to how the creator thought the puzzle could be solved.

One of the best approaches for creating a Slitherlink puzzle is to work as both a solver and a creator at the same time. As the creator makes the puzzle, he or she should think about the strategies that the solver may use for solving the puzzle. This approach also helps to ensure that a final puzzle will have a unique solution—if the creator uses logical deduction and spatial reasoning during each step of a puzzle's creation, there should be one solution to a puzzle when it is completed.

Slitherlink Worksheets

On the next two pages are two examples of Slitherlink puzzles and their solutions. Use these two examples to determine what you think the goal of a Slitherlink puzzle is and what the rules are for determining the unique solution.

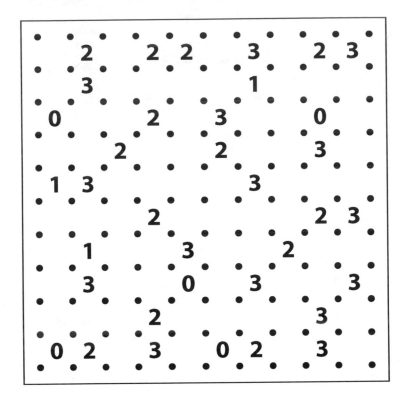

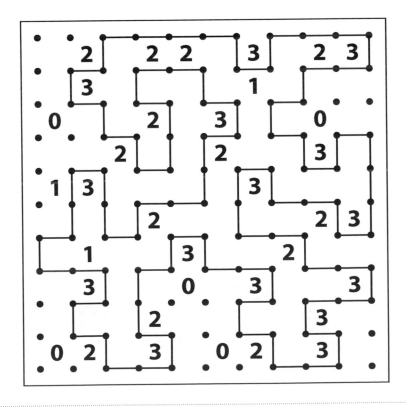

Spatial Reasoning Puzzles That Make Kids Think! © Prufrock Press Inc.

Slitherlink Worksheets

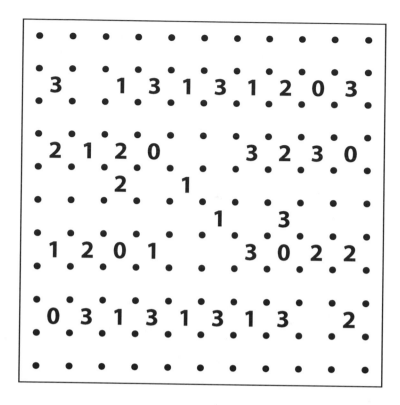

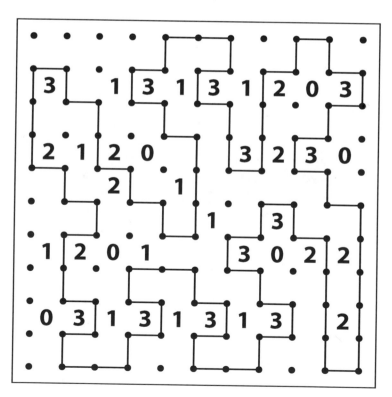

6 x 6 Slitherlink Puzzles

1

```
1 3 2 2 2 2
1 2 2 2 0 2
1 2 1 3 2 3
3 2 2 2 0 2
3 2 3 1 0 1
3 1 2 1 1 2
```

2

```
1 1 3 3 2 2
3 3 1 2 1 2
1 1 1 3 2 1
2 0 1 2 2 1
2 2 2 3 2 2
1 3 2 3 1 3
```

3

```
2 3 3 2 1 3
2 1 2 1 1 3
2 2 1 2 2 2
2 2 1 0 2 2
1 2 2 1 2 2
3 3 3 2 3 2
```

Solutions on p. 126.

4

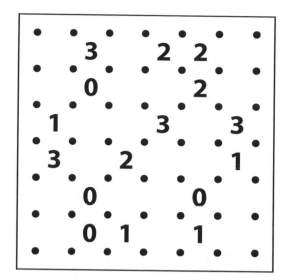

5

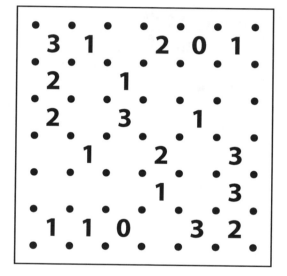

6

Solutions on p. 126.

7

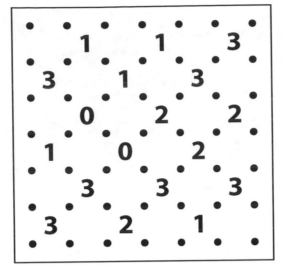

8

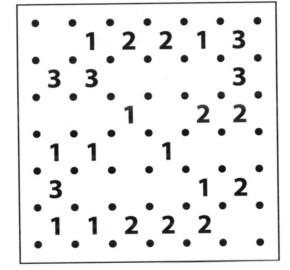

9

Solutions on p. 126.

10

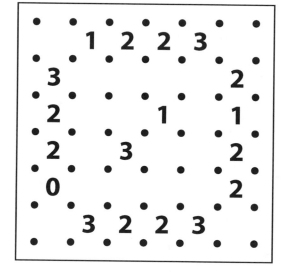

11

12

Solutions on p. 126.

8 x 8 Slitherlink Puzzles

1

```
  3 2   1 1     1 1
      3         2 3
  0 2   1 3       2
  2 2 0 0
          3 2 0 2
  1       2 0   3 2
  2 3         1
  3 2     2 2   2 3
```

2

```
  1 3   2 2 1 3 1
            0 1 2
  3 2 3
  1   1     1 2 3
  1 3 3     2     1
            2 0 1
    3 1 1
  3 2 1 1 3   2 2
```

3

```
  3 1   3 2 3     1
    2 3     2 3
    1 1       1 1
  2     1 2 3     2
  1   2 1 1       3
    3 0       1 1
    3 2       3 1
  3     1 2 1   1 2
```

Solutions on p. 127.

4

2 3 2   3 2   2
3   3 1 2 1
3   3   2
3   0 1 3
    3 1 0   2
3   1   0
2 1 1 2   1
2   2 2   1 2 3

5

    3   2 1 2
0 2 3   3 1 1
    3   2
    2   2 1   2 1
3 3   2 1   3
        1   1
2 2 1   1 3 1
    1 0 1   3

6

1 2 3   2 2 3
        0   0
    0   3   1 3 3
2   0 3   1
1   1 2   1
1 3 2   2   2
        1   2
3 1 1   1 2 2

Solutions on p. 127.

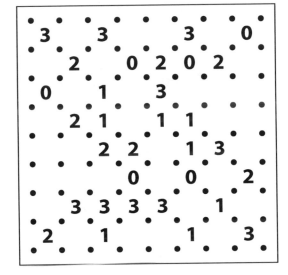

7

8

9

Solutions on p. 127.

Spatial Reasoning Puzzles That Make Kids Think! © Prufrock Press Inc.

10

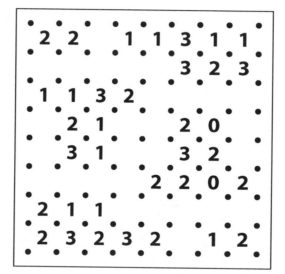

```
  1  3  2  2  1  1  2  3

  2  1     1     2     3
  2     1  2  2     3  2
  3  1     2  2  0     1
  2     2     3     3  3

  3  2  1  2  1  1  3  1
```

11

```
  2  2     1  1  3  1  1
                 3  2  3
  1  1  3  2
     2  1        2  0
     3  1        3  2
              2  2  0  2

  2  1  1
  2  3  2  3  2     1  2
```

12

```
     1        2  3  2  0
     1  2     3  0     2
  3        1        0
  2     2     1
              2     3     3
     1        2        2
  1     2  2     2  1
  2  1  1  2        3
```

Solutions on p. 127.

10 x 10 Slitherlink Puzzles

1

```
    1       0  1         3
  0  2  2      2         2  3
     3           1  0  2  3
        2              1  3
    3  3        3  2
              1  1         1  2
       2  2              0
    3  2  2  3              3
       1  0        2     2  0  3
    0              0  2      3
```

2

```
  3     2  2  2     1     2  2
  3     2  1  0           3  3
        3  1  2     2  3
  2  3              2  1
  2  2              2  3
        3  3              2  2
        2  0              3  1
        2  1     2  1  2
     1  2        3  2  2     1
     2  2     3     0  2  3     0
```

Solutions on p. 128.

3

```
0 2 2 1 3 2 2 1 1 3
1                 2
1   3 1 3 1 2 2   0
3   2         2   1
3   3   2 2 3   2
2   2   3 2 2   2
2   0         2   3
2   2 2 1 1 2 1   1
1                 0
1 3 2 1 2 2 3 1 3 1
```

4

```
1   2 3     2 2 1
              0
3     1   2 3 3   1
1   3           3 2
1       1 2 2 3
    3 3 3 3       2
2 0           3   0
3   3 2 0   1     2
  3
  2 1 1     2 0   3
```

Solutions on p. 128.

5

6

Solutions on p. 128.

7

```
 3      1  2     1  2  3
 1         0  0         1  0  3
 2  3      1        3        2
       2  3  3  2     2        2
 1                 1  0  2  1  2
 1  1  2  2  2                 2
 3     2     1  1  2  2
 1        1        2        0  2
 2  1  0        2  1           1
    2  2  2        1  1        2
```

8

```
 1  3     1  1     2  2        2
    1  3     1  0  1  2  1  2
       2     3        2  1  2
 3  2     1                    2
    3  1     3  3     2  1  1
 2  1  1     2  2     1  1
 2              1     0  2
 1  2  2     2     2
 1  2  3  1  0  2     2  3
 1     2  1     1  2     2  2
```

Solutions on p. 129.

9

```
1  0    3 1    1   3 1
3 1        0      3 1
      3    1      2
        1          2   2
   3 3   1 2 2   3   2
   1   2   2 2 1   1 1
   0   1         1
      3      2    3
 2 1      3        0 1
 2 2    2    2 1   2 2
```

10

```
 2    2    2    2 0 1
 3    0    0   1
 3    1   2     2 3 2
   2   3     1
                2 2 2
 0 2 3
      3      0    2
 2 0 1     3   1    2
      1    1    1    1
 2 1 1     1    3    3
```

Solutions on p. 129.

11

```
3     1  2  2  1  1  2     3
   2     3  3  2  0        1
 3                            2
 2           1  2             3
 2     1  2  2  3  3  2       2
 3     1  1  1  2  0  2       2
 2           2  3             2
 3                            1
    1     1  2  0  2     2
    0     3  2  2  3  2  2     1
```

12

```
 0     1  3  1  1  1        1
1  1              2     2
2  3     0           1  2  3
    2        3        0     1
    3     2     1
             2     3     3
 2     1        2        1
 0  3  2           2     1  2
    2     1           3  2
 1        1  2  2  1  3     3
```

Solutions on p. 129.

Chapter 2

◆◆◆◆◆◆◆◆◆

Hashiwokakero

◆◆◆◆◆◆◆◆◆◆◆

Another path puzzle is called Hashiwokakero, which is Japanese for "build bridges." In some publications, these puzzles are called Bridges or Chopsticks; others just abbreviate the name as Hashi. They first appeared in their current form in 1990 in the Japanese puzzle magazine *Nikoli*.

As with Slitherlink, the primary goal of a Hashiwokakero puzzle is to build a path. This time, however, the path does not need to be a closed loop—it may contain one or more closed loops, but these are not necessary (see Figures 2.1 and 2.2 for examples).

Instead, the goal is to build bridges that connect all of the islands (the circled numbers) in the grid using the following rules:

- Only vertical and horizontal line segments can be used for bridges.
- Any two islands can be connected by one bridge or two bridges (running parallel to each other).
- Bridges must start and end at islands.
- Bridges may not cross other bridges or islands.
- The number on each island must match the total number of bridges connected to that island.
- All islands must be connected—that is, you must be able to travel from each island to any other island in the grid.

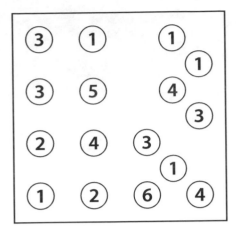

Figure 2.1. Example Hashiwokakero puzzle.

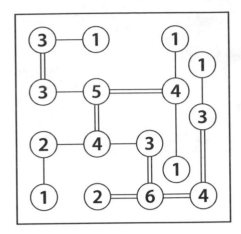

Figure 2.2. Example Hashiwokakero solution.

The solution to a Hashiwokakero puzzle is unique and can be determined using logic and spatial reasoning.

Solving the Example Puzzle

There are several different first moves that can be made in the example puzzle. A common Hashiwokakero strategy is to look for islands whose bridges can only be built in one way. For example, the 1 on the right edge has no other islands directly above, left, or right of it, so the single bridge must connect to the island below it (see Figure 2.3). Similarly, the 4 in the bottom right corner can only connect to islands above and to the left. Because no more than two bridges can be built in any direction, the bridges must be built in pairs (see Figure 2.3). Solvers often find it helpful to shade in or cross out the islands when the full number of bridges have been attached (see Figure 2.3).

When a 4 appears in a corner, there is only one way in which its bridges can be built. Likewise, if there is an island with an 8 in the middle of a puzzle, two bridges must be built in each of the four directions, or if there is an island with a 6 on the edge of a puzzle, two bridges must be built in each of the three possible directions. This is the situation on the bottom of the example puzzle (see Figure 2.4). Another special situation arises when a 3 appears in a corner. Because there are only two directions to build the bridges, then one bridge must be built in one direction and two bridges in the other. In the top left corner of the example, the 1 near the middle of the top edge determines which side of the 3 has only one bridge (see Figure 2.4).

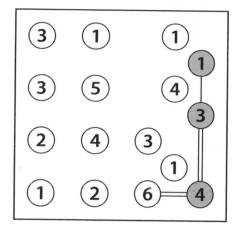

Figure 2.3. Filling in the right edge.

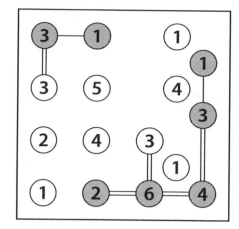

Figure 2.4. Completing the 6 and 3.

The 1 in the bottom left corner can no longer be connected to the 2 to its right (this is where the shading of completed islands is helpful), so it must have a single bridge drawn to the 2 above it (see Figure 2.5). One more bridge must be built from the 2 and there are two possible directions—above and to the right. However, if the bridge from the 2 is connected to the 3 above it, then this set of islands would be completed and could not be connected to the rest of the islands in the puzzle (see Figure 2.5). The bridge must be built to the right, connecting the 2 with the 4 and the 3 on the left must connect to the 5 on its right (see Figure 2.6).

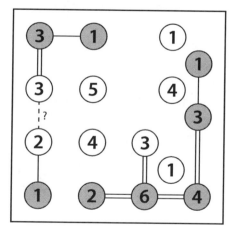

Figure 2.5. Don't let islands be disconnected from the rest.

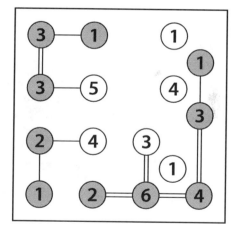

Figure 2.6. Correcting the left edge.

Now the 5 has one bridge connected to it and only two directions left in which to build bridges (to the right and down). Two bridges needs to be built on each of those sides (see Figure 2.7). The 1 near the bottom right is surrounded by bridges on three of its sides and because bridges cannot cross other bridges, a single bridge must be built connecting it to the 4 above it (see Figure 2.7). There is only one way to build each of the remaining bridges to complete the puzzle (see Figure 2.8).

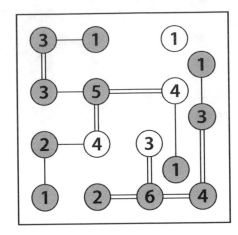
Figure 2.7. Completing the 5.

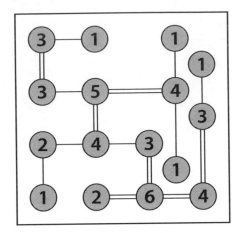
Figure 2.8. Completed puzzle.

Sometimes, in a Hashiwokakero puzzle, a first move may not be immediately obvious and a different strategy may be needed. For example, the puzzle in Figure 2.9 does not have any of the obvious starting moves—there is no 4 in a corner, 6 on an edge, or 8 in the middle. There is a 3 in each corner, but nothing immediately indicates in which direction to build one bridge and which direction to build two.

One strategy is to build bridges where you know *at least* one bridge must appear. For example, a 3 in a corner must have at least one bridge in each of the two possible directions. Likewise, a five on an edge has three possible directions for building bridges so two bridges will be built in each of two of the directions and one built in the third direction—so there is at least one in each possible direction. When these minimal numbers of bridges are built, some of the islands may be complete, like the 2 and the 1 in this example (see Figure 2.10). Additional bridges can now be added and the rest of the puzzle can be completed easily (see Figure 2.11).

Figure 2.9. Where to start.

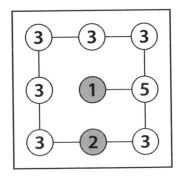
Figure 2.10. Minimal bridges.

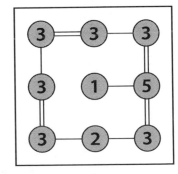
Figure 2.11. Completed puzzle.

Creating Hashiwokakero Puzzles

The first thing to notice about creating Hashiwokakero puzzles is how the circles are arranged in columns and rows. The puzzles are classified by the total number of columns and rows that could contain the circles (Figure 2.1 is a 7x7 puzzle and Figure 2.9 is a 5x5 puzzle). Circles could appear in any of the underlying grid squares (see Figure 2.12)—but never immediately adjacent, as there must be at least a space of one unit for the bridges.

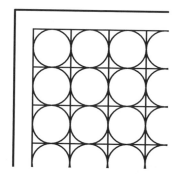

Figure 2.12. Underlying grid of squares and circles.

In some Hashiwokakero puzzles, the circles are arranged in a design that has 180° rotational symmetry (see Figure 2.13). Notice that the pattern of circles has symmetry, but not the numbers themselves (e.g., the 3 at the top left corresponds with a 2 at the bottom right). If the pattern of numbers was also symmetric, then the solution path would be symmetric too, and the solver would only have to solve half of the puzzle. Instead, the asymmetry of the numbers leads to a solution path that is not symmetric (see Figure 2.14). Hashiwokakero puzzles with circles that are in a symmetric pattern are more difficult to create than ones that do not have symmetry—it is often difficult to connect all of the islands without making the solution path symmetric. Puzzle creators are encouraged to start with asymmetric grids and then to challenge themselves with symmetric grids once they become more familiar with making these puzzles.

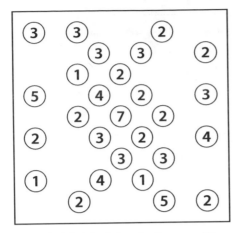

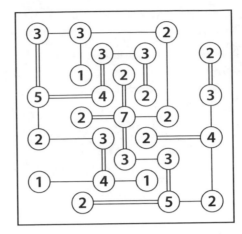

Figure 2.13. Hashiwokakero with symmetry.

Figure 2.14. Asymmetrical solution.

More importantly, puzzle creators should make use of deductive and spatial reasoning when creating their puzzles. They should create their puzzles using various solving strategies like those described previously.

Puzzle creators must be careful to avoid situations that lead to multiple solutions. These can arise when a closed loop is embedded in a puzzle. A simple example is shown in Figure 2.15.

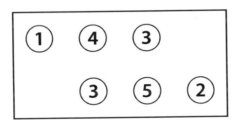

Figure 2.15. Not a good puzzle.

When the bridge is built from the 1 to the 4 and the two bridges are built from the 2 to the 5, that leaves three bridges that need to be built from each of the remaining numbers. This situation leads to two different solutions (see Figure 2.16). It is important for puzzle creators to check their puzzles to avoid multiple solutions like the ones in Figure 2.16.

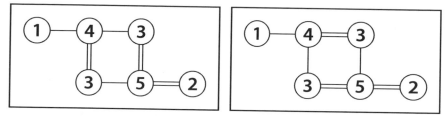

Figure 2.16. Two solutions.

A Hashiwokakero puzzle creator often starts with a blank grid of squares and fills in circles and numbers as the puzzle is constructed, making sure that the solution path connects all of the circles and that various solution strategies are utilized throughout the puzzle. Puzzles with lots of large and small numbers are sometimes easier to solve than ones with lots of threes, fours, and fives, but it is the placement of these numbers relative to each other and to the grid that determines a puzzle's overall difficulty.

After a puzzle has been designed on a grid, the puzzle creator can remove the grid, leaving behind the circles and numbers for solving. This can be done by tracing the circles and numbers onto a piece of paper that has been placed on top of the grid. If the puzzle is designed electronically, the process of removing the grid can be even easier.

Hashiwokakero Worksheets

On the next two pages are two examples of Hashiwokakero puzzles and their solutions. Use these two examples to determine what you think the goal of a Hashiwokakero puzzle is and what the rules are for determining the unique solution.

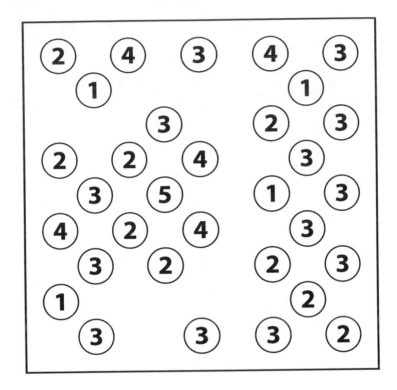

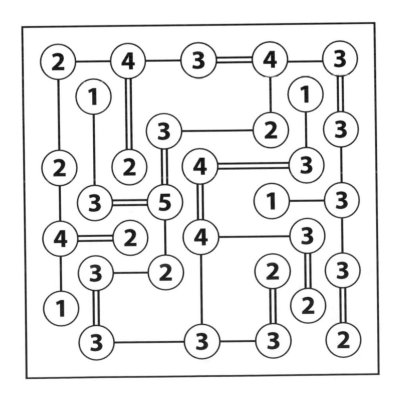

Hashiwokakero Worksheets

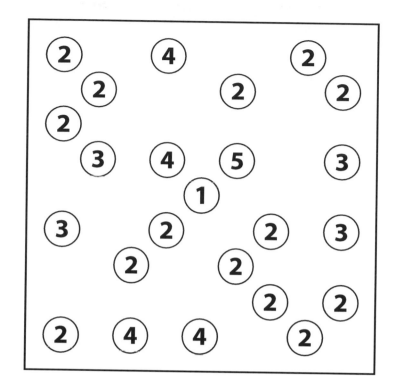

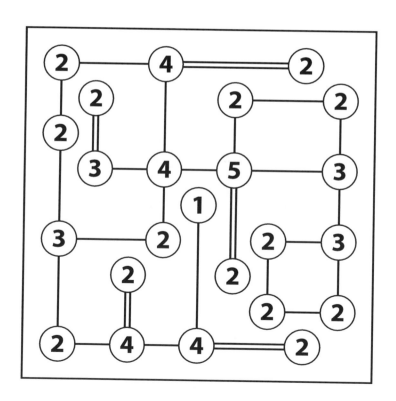

7 x 7 Hashiwokakero Puzzles

1

```
┌──────────────────────────────────┐
│   ①   ③   ①                      │
│  ③   ③   ①   ③                   │
│                                    │
│         ①                         │
│  ②        ④        ⑤             │
│                                    │
│         ①              ②         │
└──────────────────────────────────┘
```

2

```
┌──────────────────────────────────┐
│  ③       ②           ③          │
│                                    │
│  ④           ④       ⑥          │
│                                    │
│  ②   ②       ④       ⑥          │
│                                    │
│  ③           ④       ③          │
└──────────────────────────────────┘
```

3

```
┌──────────────────────────────────┐
│  ①   ④              ④            │
│                  ②                │
│         ②                         │
│                  ⑥    ⑤          │
│  ③   ①                           │
│                  ②                │
│  ②       ②           ②          │
└──────────────────────────────────┘
```

Solutions on p. 130.

4

```
2        2        1
              1
6        4        2

4    4    6    4

2    2    1    1
```

5

```
1    2        3

3    2    3    3

4    2    5    4

2    4    5    1
```

6

```
2        1        3
      3        1
         1        5

3    7        6

1    3    2    4
```

Solutions on p. 130.

7

②	①	②
③	③	③
④	④ ④	④
	①	
③	④ ①	③ ①

8

③	⑤	④	④
	②	③	
	②	③	③
④	①		
	②	④	②
③		②	
	①	③	③

9

①	③	①
①		①
③		①
④	⑥	②
③	①	③
②		
②	⑤	③

Solutions on p. 130.

Spatial Reasoning Puzzles That Make Kids Think! © Prufrock Press Inc.

10

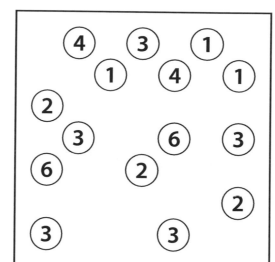

11

12

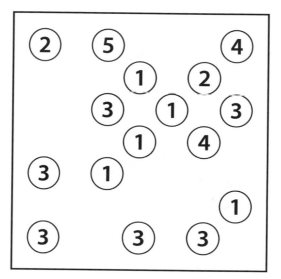

Solutions on p. 130.

9 x 9 Hashiwokakero Puzzles

1

```
 1        1
    1        1   3
       2
 3  3      3   4

       2   3

 3
    2      3   3
 2
```

2

```
 2   1      3   1
    1   4   1

 4      5   3   1


          2   1
 1        2   4

 1      4   4   3
```

Solutions on p. 131.

3

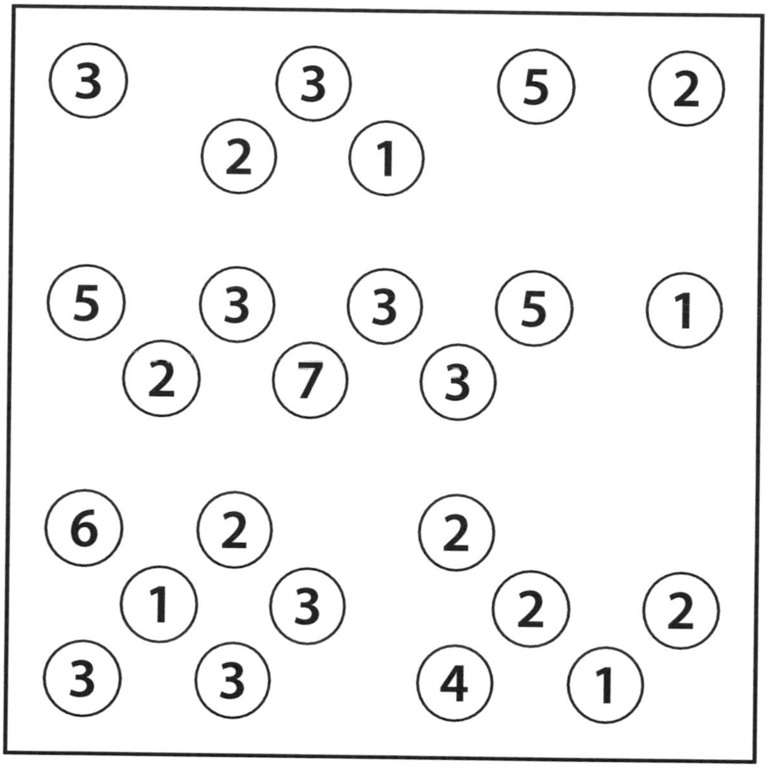

③ ③ ⑤ ②
② ①

⑤ ③ ③ ⑤ ①
② ⑦ ③

⑥ ② ②
① ③ ② ②
③ ③ ④ ①

4

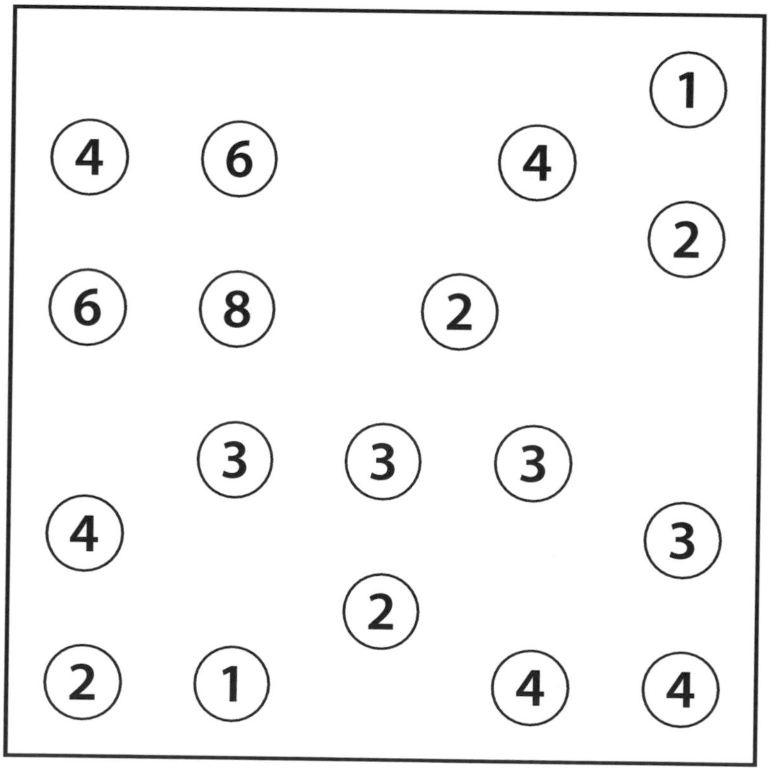

①
④ ⑥ ④
②
⑥ ⑧ ②

③ ③ ③
④ ③
②
② ① ④ ④

Solutions on p. 131.

5

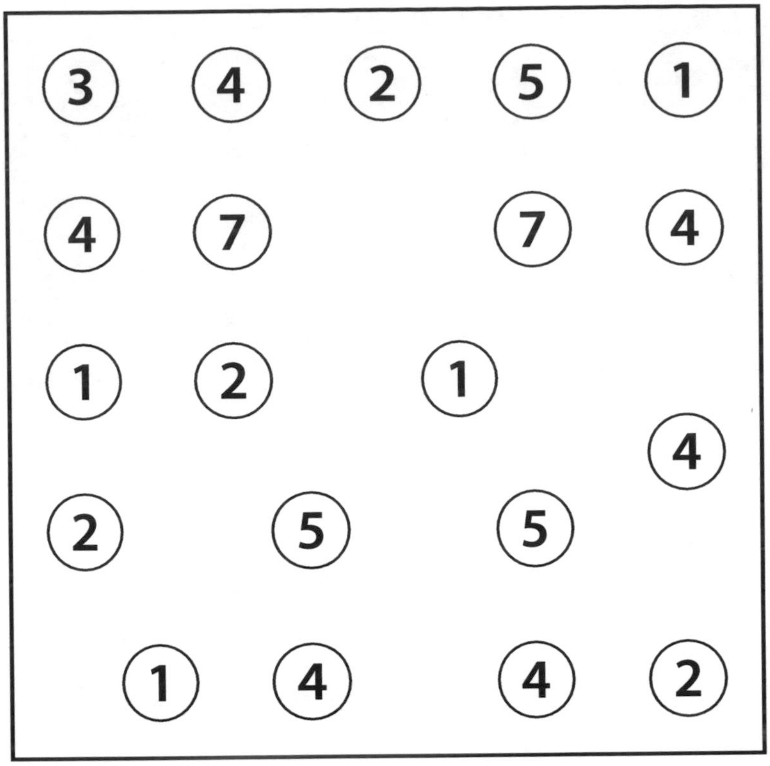

③ ④ ② ⑤ ①

④ ⑦ ⑦ ④

① ② ①

④

② ⑤ ⑤

① ④ ④ ②

6

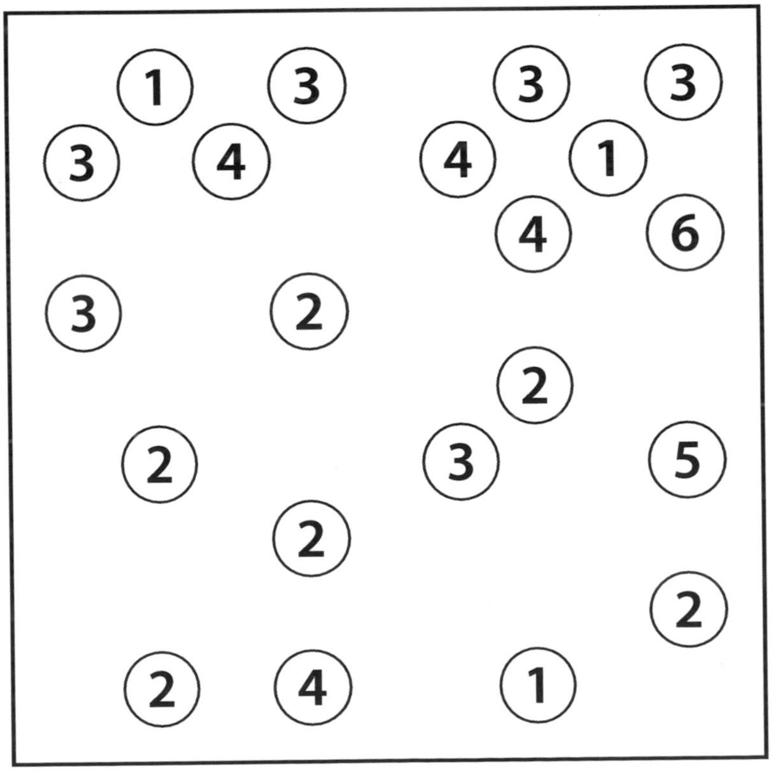

① ③ ③ ③

③ ④ ④ ①

④ ⑥

③ ②

②

② ③ ⑤

②

②

② ④ ①

Solutions on p. 131.

7

```
  1         1    1    3

  4         6         6


            2

  6           4         4


       2        4    1
  2          2    4    3
```

8

```
  2    4       5       3

            1

  2           3    1

            3           3

       2          2

  3    3    2    3    4

  1    1    1         3
```

Solutions on p. 131.

9

```
 2    1    1    5    4

 6    6         6    4

           1

 3

      1    4    4    1

 1

    1         2    1
```

10

```
      1         4         3

 4              2

      1              3    1

 5                   4         5

           2

      2         3         2

           3         2         5

 4    5         2         1

    2         3    3         4
```

Solutions on p. 131.

11

12

Solutions on p. 131.

16 x 9 Hashiwokakero Puzzles

1

(2)   (2)   (4)   (5)   (2)   (5)   (4)

(2)   (3)   (2)   (3)

(6)   (5)   (4)   (4)   (7)   (4)

(1)   (2)   (3)   (1)

(3)   (3)   (3)

(2)   (5)   (2)

(1)   (4)   (2)   (2)

2

(2)   (4)   (4)   (5)   (4)   (3)

(2)   (4)   (8)   (6)   (4)

(2)

(2)   (3)   (2)

(1)   (4)   (5)   (2)

(2)   (2)   (1)   (2)   (8)   (4)   (3)

(1)   (3)

(1)   (3)   (3)   (2)   (3)   (3)

Solutions on p. 132.

3

2   3   4   2   3   1
1
3   3   1   3   6   5   1
3   1
2   6   2   2   3   1
4   4   6   3   5   2
4   2   3   3   2

4

1   1   2   3   2   2   1
3   4   4   3   5   3
4   1   2   4   2   5
1   7   2   2
2   4   4   4   2   2

Solutions on p. 132.

5

② ④ ④ ② ⑤ ⑤ ③
②
② ③ ③
④ ② ③ ② ⑥ ⑤
④ ⑥ ②
② ① ⑤ ④
② ① ① ③
② ⑤ ③ ④ ③ ③

6

① ② ⑤ ④ ③ ④ ④
⑤ ④ ②
④ ④ ⑤ ⑤
② ⑤ ③ ①
① ⑦ ③ ②
⑥ ⑤ ② ③ ①
①
④ ⑤ ⑤ ④ ④ ②

Solutions on p. 132.

7

2 5 3   3 4   2
                          1
1 4   3   5 1

4 6   6   5   5 2
2 4   2 2   2
2 2
3 4   3   4 3
2 4 3   5 6 6   3

8

4 4   3   4   4 4 3
      2   1   1 1 2
                  2 2 4
4 4   5 4 5 6
  2 5 2   4
3   2
4 2 1 5   4
1 2 4 1   2 2 2
  1 1 3 4   1 3 4

Solutions on p. 133.

9

③ ① ④ ③ ② ① ① ③
③ ③ ② ③ ④ ③
③ ③ ③ ④
① ③ ④
② ④ ③ ①
② ⑤ ⑧ ⑤
③
③ ⑤ ④ ② ④ ①
② ② ③ ③ ③

10

② ② ④ ③ ⑤ ③
①
② ④ ③
⑤ ⑤ ② ③
① ② ③
② ② ⑥ ④
②
② ② ② ④ ④
② ③ ④ ③ ③ ② ③ ④

Solutions on p. 133.

11

```
3   4   3   3           3   2   1
  2   4   3
3   2   2   5             4       4

2   1   1       3     3   1   3
  4   6                     3   2
2   1   4   5     2   4   1   1
                       2   3   1
1   5     5   6     3   4   3
```

12

```
          2   4     4   4   4   3
3   5       6     6       5   1
      2             2   2
1           1   3   1   3       3
      3   5   3   3   1
4   6   2             5     5   5
      3         3               1
3   3               1   2   2
      3         4   5   4   3
```

Solutions on p. 133.

Chapter 3

Masyu

The path puzzle known as Masyu was also developed by the Japanese puzzle magazine *Nikoli*. It first appeared in 1998 using only white circles in the grids. By 2000, the puzzle was changed to include both white and black circles. Masyu puzzles are truly language-independent logic puzzles as they do not use any numbers or letters in the puzzle grids.

The name Masyu loosely translates as "evil influence" in Japanese. This name actually came from a misreading of the original Japanese name for "white pearls and black pearls," but the name became an inside joke at *Nikoli* and has since stuck.

The goal of a Masyu puzzle is to create a path made up of horizontal and vertical line segments that is a closed loop, traveling through every white and black circle. The behavior of the path as it travels through the white and black circles is what makes Masyu stand out from any other path puzzle. See the two example puzzles (see Figures 3.1 and 3.3) and their solutions (see Figures 3.2 and 3.4).

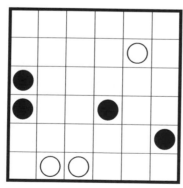

Figure 3.1. Example Masyu puzzle A.

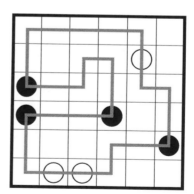

Figure 3.2. Example Masyu solution A.

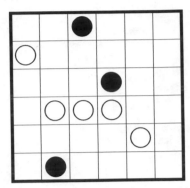

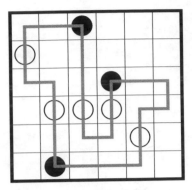

Figure 3.3. Example Masyu puzzle B.

Figure 3.4. Example Masyu solution B.

The rules for solving Masyu puzzles are:
- **White circles:** As the path travels through white circles, it must go straight through, but it must turn immediately in the next square on at least one side of the circle.
- **Black circles:** As the path travels through black circles, it must make a right-angle turn and go straight through the first square on both sides of the circle.

These are the only two rules for solving Masyu puzzles—keeping in mind the goal of making one closed loop. Even though there are only two rules, it is easy for the novice solver to overlook a rule when solving a Masyu puzzle. As with all logic puzzles, the solutions are unique, the knowledge of which can be a helpful strategy in solving Masyu puzzles.

Solving the Example Puzzles

Each of the two example puzzles presents some unique situations and requires some different strategies that will be helpful in tackling and creating other puzzles. Example A has two white circles adjacent to each other along an edge. Because the path must travel straight through each white circle and turn on at least one side of each white circle, there is only one way that the path can be drawn—through both white circles and into the center on both ends (see Figure 3.5). There are also two black circles adjacent to each other along the left edge of the puzzle. Because the path must turn in each black circle and travel straight through the first square on both sides of the circle, there is only one way that the path can be drawn—into the center and away from the black circles (see Figure 3.6).

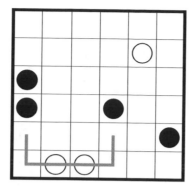

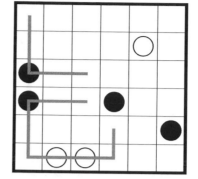

Figure 3.5. Two white circles.   Figure 3.6. Two black circles.

The path can also travel in only two directions from the black circle near the bottom right corner of the puzzle. Because it must travel completely through one square on both sides of the turn, it must travel left and up from the circle (see Figure 3.7). The same argument can now be made with the black circle near the center of the grid—because the path cannot travel down and right, it must travel left and up (see Figure 3.8).

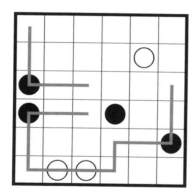

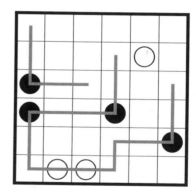

Figure 3.7. Bottom right corner.   Figure 3.8. Black circle near the
                                      center.

As the path travels through the remaining white circle near the top right corner, it is either a straight horizontal or a vertical line segment. If the path were horizontal, it would force the loop to close on the right side of the grid without connecting to the rest of the path (see Figure 3.9). This means that instead, the path must travel vertically through the white circle, connecting to the existing path below and to the right (see Figure 3.10).

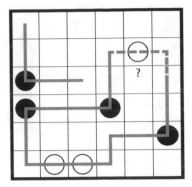

Figure 3.9. Don't close the loop too soon.

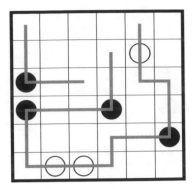

Figure 3.10. Vertical path through the white circle.

Three of the path ends are in places where the path must turn and there is only one way for each one to go (see Figure 3.11). To keep the path from closing again on the right, the two ends in the second row must connect, leaving the two ends on the top row to also connect in a straight line (see Figure 3.12).

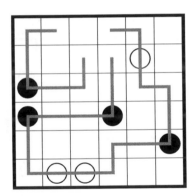

Figure 3.11. Turning at the ends.

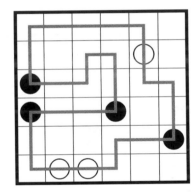

Figure 3.12. Connecting the ends.

Example B features three white circles in a row. Considering the middle circle, if the path were to travel horizontally through it, it would have to continue to travel horizontally through the circles on either side of it (see Figure 3.13). This violates the rule that states that the path must turn on at least one side of every white circle. Therefore, the path must travel vertically through the middle circle, which forces the path also to travel vertically through the other two white circles (see Figure 3.14). This approach is very useful in puzzles when white circles appear in a line of three or more.

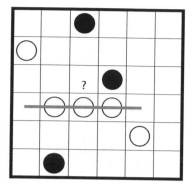

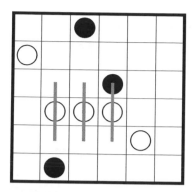

Figure 3.13. Don't forget about the middle circle.

Figure 3.14. Correctly tackling a line of white circles.

The path must also travel vertically through the white circle on the left side of the grid (see Figure 3.15). Looking at the black circle at the bottom of the grid, the path cannot travel left or down, so it must travel right and up (see Figure 3.15). Continuing with the path through the white circle on the left edge, it must turn to the right on both ends, joining with another part of the path below it (see Figure 3.16). And looking at the black circle near the middle of the grid, the path must turn either to the left or to the right. It cannot turn to the left because it must travel completely through one full square, and in this case, it would run through another part of the path. Therefore, it must turn to the right.

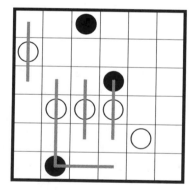

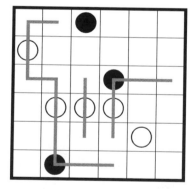

Figure 3.15. White circle along an edge.

Figure 3.16. Finishing at the left edge.

The path through the black circle at the top must extend down into the middle of the grid, connecting to another part of the path that is already there. The path also has to turn to the right below the set of three white circles (see Figure 3.17). It must also travel either left or right through the black circle at the top of the grid. If it extends to the right, that would leave an end in the top right corner blocked in. Therefore, the path must travel to the left (see Figure 3.17).

The remaining white circle near the bottom right corner cannot contain a horizontal path segment (it would run into the corner of the path to its left), so it must contain a vertical path segment. The ends of this segment are then connected to the existing path to complete the closed loop solution to the puzzle (see Figure 3.18).

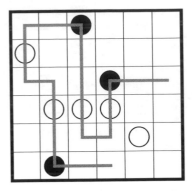

Figure 3.17. Connecting at the top.

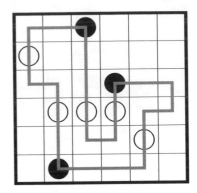

Figure 3.18. The final circle.

It is not uncommon for the solution to a Masyu puzzle to develop in pieces, as demonstrated in both of these examples. Using deductive and spatial reasoning, the closed loop can be determined as the separate pieces come together in the final stages of the puzzle.

Creating Masyu Puzzles

The most important thing about creating Masyu puzzles is that the creator needs to know the pathway rules for both the white and black circles very well. It is easy to overlook a small aspect of one of the rules and to create a puzzle that has more than one solution.

One approach to creating a Masyu puzzle is to draw a path and then place black and white circles on the path throughout the grid where appropriate. This approach is not a good one to take for several reasons. First, if all of the possible circle locations are marked, the entire path may be almost unmistakably outlined (see Figure 3.19) and the puzzle may be too easy to solve (see Figure 3.20). A number of the circles in Figure 3.19 can be removed to create the same solution and a puzzle that is a little more challenging to solve.

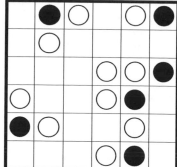

Figure 3.19. Too many circles.

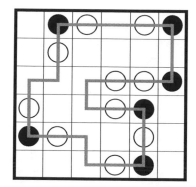

Figure 3.20. Predictable solution.

Second, a path may be created that is impossible to define using black and white circles. In the example in Figure 3.21, every possible circle is placed on the path, but the middle section with the short turns cannot be completely defined in the open space (see Figure 3.22), leaving multiple possible solutions. If this situation arises, the creator may be able to abandon the original intended solution, and add at least one additional circle to the grid to force a different unique solution.

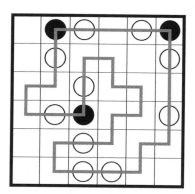

Figure 3.21. Intended solution.

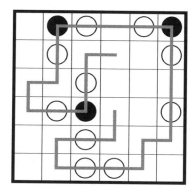

Figure 3.22. Open space leads to many solutions.

A better approach is to create a puzzle while simultaneously solving it. That is, the creator should design a puzzle by filling in pieces of the path using logic and reasoning. This way, the creator can make sure that there is exactly one solution and that there is a way for the solver to deduce the solution.

Puzzle designers can also decide on a theme for a puzzle before creating it. Masyu themes can involve specific solving strategies and situations, arrangements of circles or the path, or limitations on the circles that are used. For example, the puzzle in Figure 3.23 was designed only to use white circles. It has a unique solution (see Figure 3.24) and requires the solver to practice some specific strategies involving white circles.

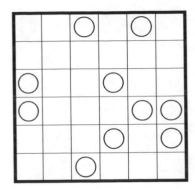

Figure 3.23. White circles only.

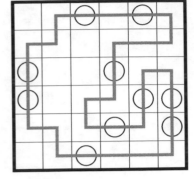

Figure 3.24. White circles solution.

Whatever strategy is used to create a Masyu puzzle, it is standard practice not to have a puzzle with a solution path that has rotational symmetry. And as with any other type of puzzle, it is important to check the solution for uniqueness.

Masyu Worksheets

On the next two pages are two examples of Masyu puzzles and their solutions. Use these two examples to determine what you think the goal of a Masyu puzzle is and what the rules are for determining the unique solution.

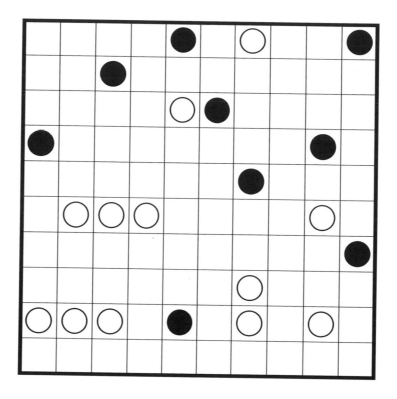

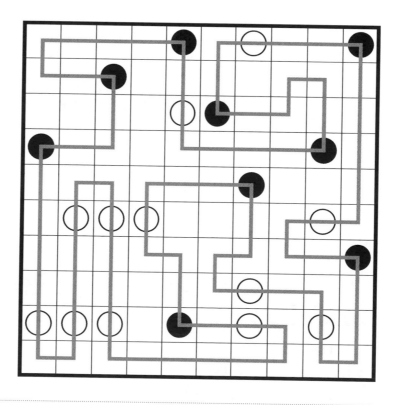

Masyu Worksheets

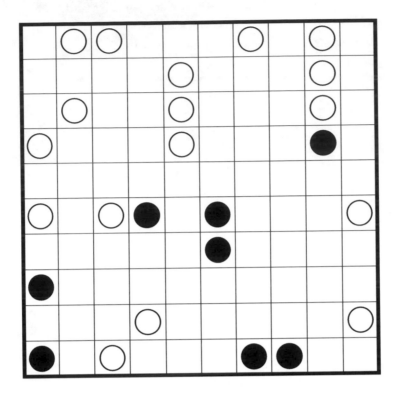

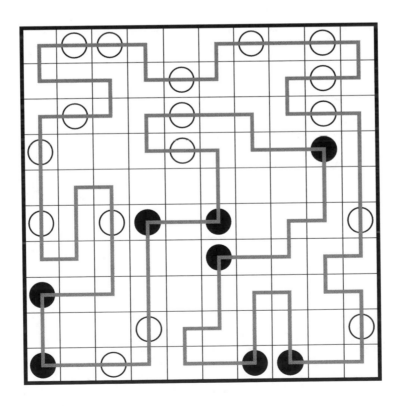

Spatial Reasoning Puzzles That Make Kids Think! © Prufrock Press Inc.

6 x 6 Masyu Puzzles

1

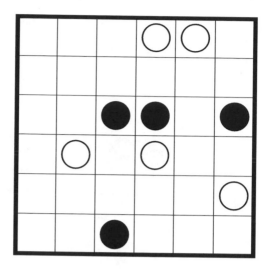

2

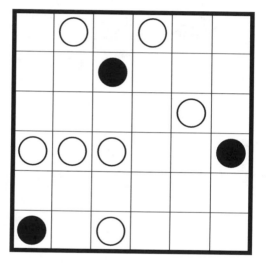

3

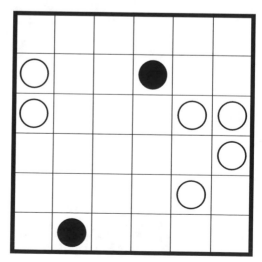

Solutions on p. 134.

4

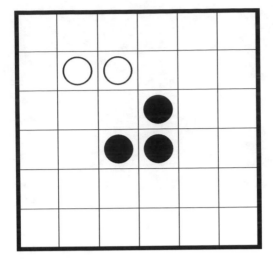

5

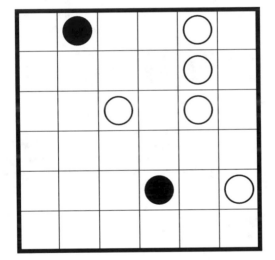

6

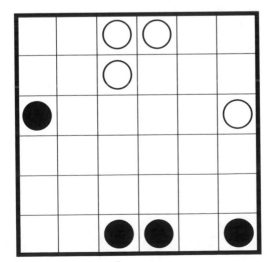

Solutions on p. 134.

7

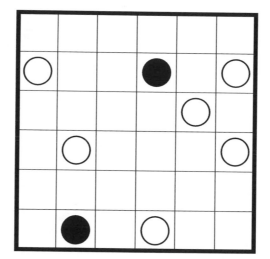

8

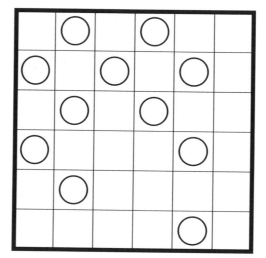

9

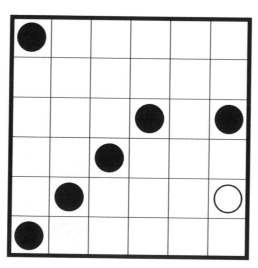

Solutions on p. 134.

10

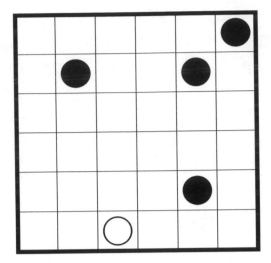

11

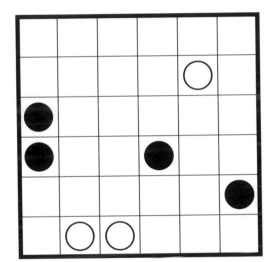

12

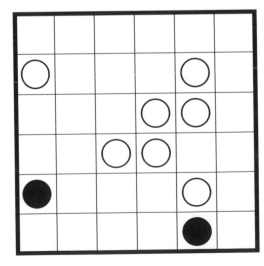

Solutions on p. 134.

8 x 8 Masyu Puzzles

1

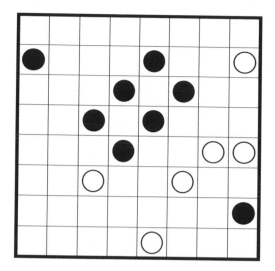

2

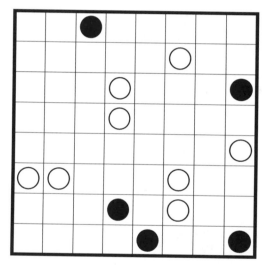

3

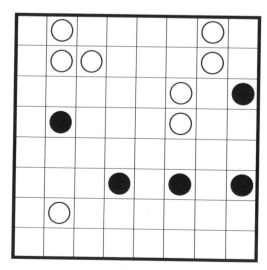

Solutions on p. 135.

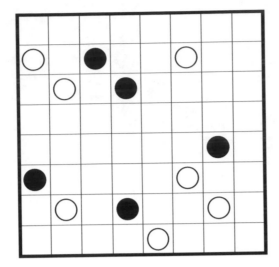

4

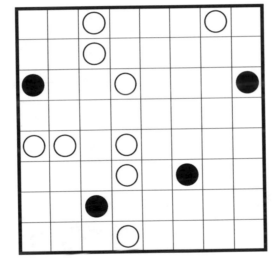

5

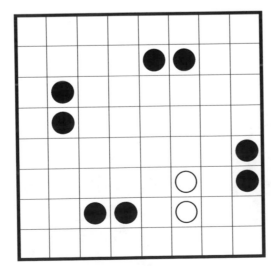

6

Solutions on p. 135.

7

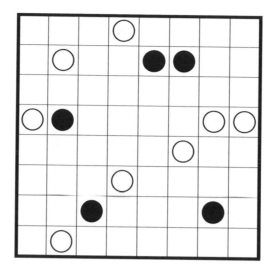

8

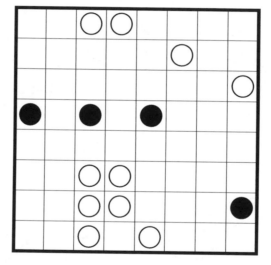

9

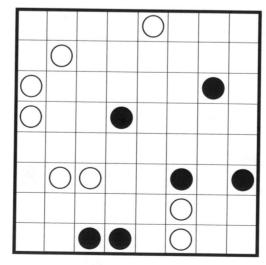

Solutions on p. 135.

10

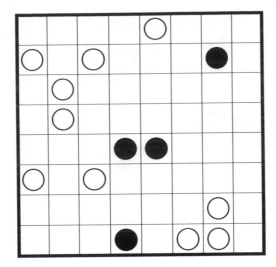

11

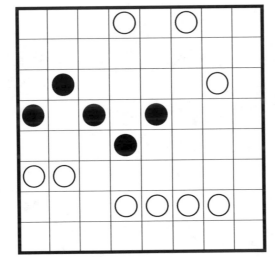

12

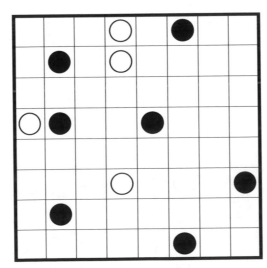

Solutions on p. 135.

10 x 10 Masyu Puzzles

1

2

Solutions on p. 136.

③

④

Solutions on p. 136.

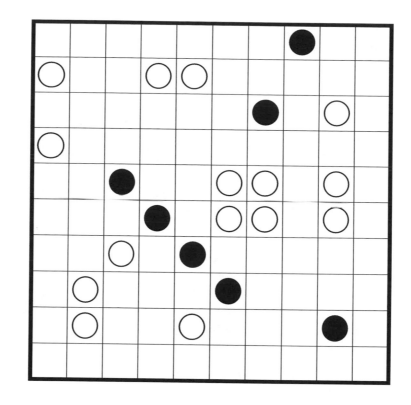

5

6

7

8

Solutions on p. 137.

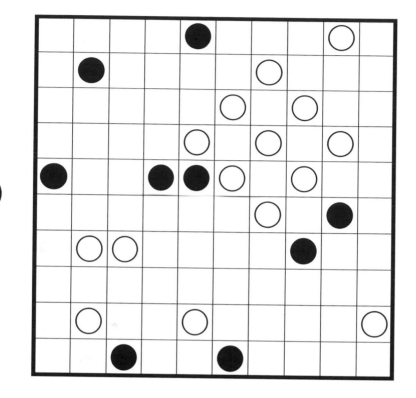

11

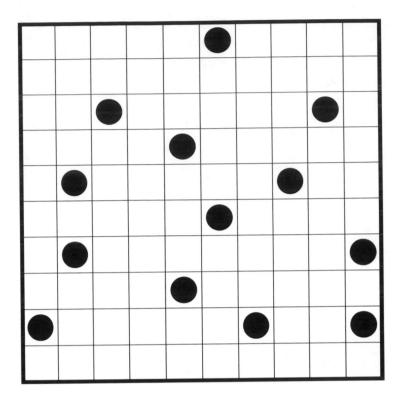

12

Solutions on p. 137.

Spatial Reasoning Puzzles That Make Kids Think! © Prufrock Press Inc.

Chapter 4

Yajilin

In 1999, the Japanese puzzle magazine *Nikoli* introduced another path puzzle known as Yajilin, which also has been published under the name Arrow Ring.

The starting grid for a Yajilin puzzle has some boxes that contain both an arrow and a number (see the examples in Figures 4.1 and 4.3). In the solution, every box in the grid will contain either: (1) an arrow and number, (2) a black square, or (3) part of the solution path—a closed loop (see the solutions to the examples in Figures 4.2 and 4.4). Each number indicates how many black squares lie in the direction indicated by the accompanying arrow. The only remaining rule for determining the solution to a Yajilin puzzle is that two black squares cannot touch horizontally or vertically.

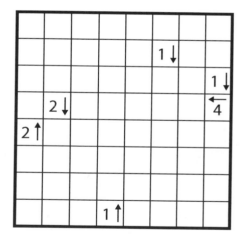

Figure 4.1. Example Yajilin Puzzle 1.

Figure 4.2. Example Yajilin solution 1.

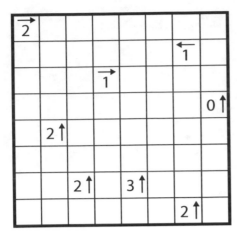

Figure 4.3. Example Yajilin Puzzle 2.

Figure 4.4. Example Yajilin solution 2.

It is important to note that a black square may be defined by more than one arrow. For example, in Figure 4.4, the black square in the second box of the top row is defined by the arrow to its left and the arrow below it. A black square may also appear in a solution grid that is not defined by any arrow. For example, in Figure 4.4, the two black squares in the two bottom rows of the grid do not have any arrows pointing at them. A puzzle's black squares and the unique solution path are determined using logic and spatial reasoning with the Yajilin rules.

Solving the Example Puzzles

Example 1

One of the easiest places to start in a Yajilin puzzle is with a number indicating black squares that can only be placed in one possible way. For example, if a 2 is pointing at three boxes, the black squares have to be placed in the first and third boxes (because black squares cannot be horizontally adjacent). If a 3 is pointing at five boxes, the black squares have to be placed in the first, third, and fifth boxes. And if a 4 is pointing at seven boxes, the black squares have to be placed in the first, third, fifth, and seventh boxes (see Figure 4.5). Because the boxes between these black squares cannot be filled with black squares, they must either contain an arrow or part of the path. The two that do not contain an arrow must be used for the path, so vertical segments are drawn through these boxes (see Figure 4.5).

The boxes above the first and fourth black squares present a similar situation—they cannot be black squares and they do not contain an arrow, so they must be part of the path. However, because they are each bounded on two sides (by a black square, an edge of the grid, or a box with an arrow), the path must turn in each of these boxes (see Figure 4.6). The box on the left side of the grid indicating two black squares above it forces a black square to be filled in the top left corner (see Figure 4.6).

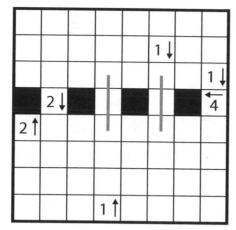

Figure 4.5. Four black squares.

Figure 4.6. Example Yajilin solution 1.

The square in the top left corner helps define more of the path. The boxes below and to the right of this square must also contain the path as it makes a turn, so the path can be extended (see Figure 4.7). Likewise, the second and third black squares in the fourth row also define parts of the path as it turns above these squares (see Figure 4.7). The path in the top left corner of the grid is in danger of closing off the loop too soon (before the rest of the grid is filled). Each of the ends is extended to the right to avoid closing the loop (see Figure 4.8).

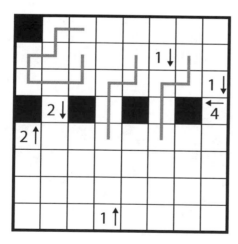

Figure 4.7. More path turns.

Figure 4.8. Avoiding closing the loop.

The two white boxes in the top right corner must either both be part of the path, or they must both be shaded black. Because two black squares cannot be adjacent to each other, they must be part of the path (see Figure 4.9). The 2 with an arrow pointing down in the fourth row indicates that two of the boxes below it must contain black squares. If the box in the bottom row were shaded black, the squares on either side would be dead-ends for the path. Similarly, if the box two rows below the 2 with an arrow pointing down were shaded black, the boxes above it and to its left would be dead-ends for the path (see Figure 4.10).

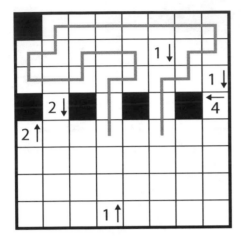

Figure 4.9. Completing the top right corner.

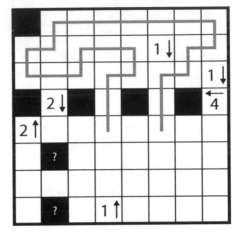

Figure 4.10. Avoiding dead-end paths.

Instead, the other two boxes in the second column must be shaded black and the path drawn around these black squares (see Figure 4.11). There is only one unused box above the 1 in the bottom row, so it must be shaded black, extending the path below it (see Figure 4.12). The third and fourth black squares in the fourth now force parts of the path to turn below them (see Figure 4.12).

Figure 4.11. Completing the bottom left corner.

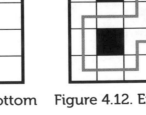

Figure 4.12. Extending the path.

On the right side of the grid, the path must continue down two squares (to avoid closing the loop), leaving the square in the bottom right corner to be shaded black, as indicated by the 1 on the right side of the grid (see Figure 4.13). The path must also turn above and to the left of this black square (see Figure 4.13). To keep the path from reaching a dead-end, there is only one box for the remaining black square indicated by the 1 with the arrow pointing down in the second row. This box is shaded black and the rest of the path is filled in (see Figure 4.14).

Figure 4.13. Completing the bottom right corner.

Figure 4.14. The completed solution.

Example 2

At first glance, the second example puzzle doesn't appear to have as obvious of a start for finding the solution path. However, a few different strategies can be very helpful for solving this puzzle. For example, the placement of the 0 in the grid may not be useful in locating any black squares, but it does indicate where part of the path is located. Because the set of three squares above the 0 includes two boxes that must contain a turn, the path must travel around the top right corner of the grid (see Figure 4.15). Also, the 2 in the bottom row forces a black square to be placed in the bottom right corner, which indicates that another part of the path turns above this square in the bottom right corner of the grid (see Figure 4.15).

The 2 in the top row demonstrates an important situation that often arises in Yajilin puzzles. Because two black squares must be placed along the top edge of the grid and there are four remaining boxes that could be used, there is only one placement of the two black squares that will prevent a path from reaching a dead-end between the two black squares. They must be placed at both ends of the line of four open boxes, creating a U-turn for the path between them (see Figure 4.16). The path can also be extended in a few spots where it now must make a turn (see Figure 4.16).

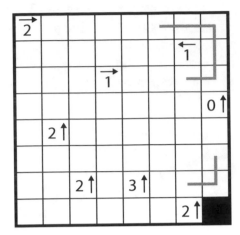

Figure 4.15. Completing the bottom right corner.

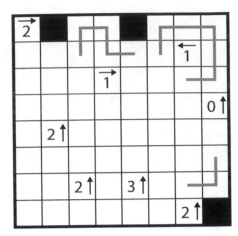

Figure 4.16. Completing the top row.

There are now several black squares that can be placed using some of the numbers in the grid. The 2 in the bottom row points toward three open boxes, so the two black squares must be placed with an open box between them (see Figure 4.17). The second row contains a 1 that is pointing at two open boxes, but only the one at the far left is not adjacent to an existing black square (see Figure 4.17). With these three additional black squares in place, more parts of the path can be drawn (see Figure 4.17).

In the top right corner of the grid, there is a loop that could be closed too early, so the path must extend to the left to avoid this (see Figure 4.18). The 2 in the second column indicates that another black square must be placed above the 2 in this column. A black square is placed in the one remaining box, and the path is extended down the left side of the grid (see Figure 4.18).

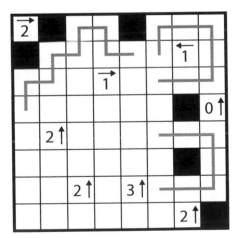

Figure 4.17. Three more black squares.

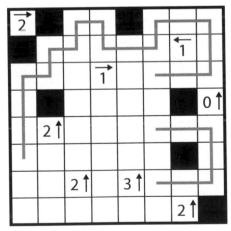

Figure 4.18. Extending the path on the left side.

The 2 near the bottom of the third column indicates that two black squares must be placed above it. One has to go in the third row to keep the path from reaching a dead-end (see Figure 4.19). The second black square must be placed directly above the 2, leaving two boxes between them for another U-turn (see Figure 4.19). The 1 in the third row forces a black square to placed in the remaining open box, creating a turn in the path on its right (see Figure 4.19).

Along the bottom row, the two open boxes at the right present an interesting situation. If a black square were to be placed in either one of them, the path would be forced to reach a dead-end in the other. This means that the path must travel through both of them (see Figure 4.20). The two black squares in the second column from the right now help to create turns in the pieces of the path on their left (see Figure 4.20).

Figure 4.19. Another U-turn.

Figure 4.20. Extending the path on the bottom.

The 3 in the fifth column forces a black square to be placed in the remaining open box above it, connecting parts of the path in several places (see Figure 4.21). On the left side of the grid, the path must turn next to the black square near the bottom of the third column (see Figure 4.21).

The open box between the 2 and the 3 in the second row from the bottom must contain a black square. This, along with the black square in the bottom right corner, shows how a black square may be placed in a grid without a number and arrow pointing at it (see Figure 4.22). When the path is extended along the bottom, the two remaining open boxes in the bottom left corner must also contain part of the path (because they can't both contain black squares), so the puzzle is completed by joining the closed loop (see Figure 4.22).

Figure 4.21. Satisfying the 3.

Figure 4.22. The completed solution.

Creating Yajilin Puzzles

One of the best ways to start creating Yajilin puzzles is to use some of the same beginning solving strategies from puzzles that have already been solved. Puzzle designers often use similar starting positions to get a solver engaged in a puzzle and then introduce other elements to make the puzzle unique. As with other puzzle types, corners and edges are often good places to start.

For example, in Figure 4.23, this puzzle uses two common corner strategies—alternating black squares near the top left corner and avoiding a dead-end in the bottom right corner. In each of these cases, there is only one possible placement for pieces of the path and the designer can fill these in to determine as much of the path as possible. The puzzle designer may not yet know where the entire path will go, but this gives the designer a starting point to work with (see Figure 4.24).

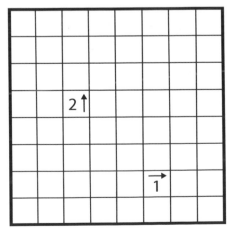

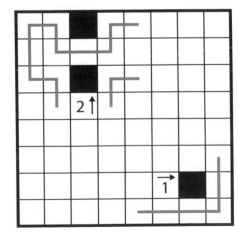

Figure 4.23. Designing from the corners.

Figure 4.24. Filling in the path.

Once pieces of a path have been placed, the designer can continue to fill in clues that determine additional pieces of the path. The placement of the additional clues must not create situations that do not allow for a complete solution or for multiple solutions. For example, placing a clue at the right end of the fourth row so that there are three black squares to the left looks, at first, to be a good possibility—there is only one placement of three black squares that might work (see Figure 4.25). However, when the path pieces are drawn in (see Figure 4.26), the remaining grid has now been divided into two open regions—the top right and the bottom—each of which has an odd number of path ends (three in the top right and five in the bottom). Because an even number of path ends must exist in each region to make a closed loop, this puzzle is now unsolvable and must be either discarded or the last clue needs to be changed (this is usually the better option).

Another similar situation that must be avoided occurs when the endpoint of a path is needed to do two different things at the same time. This often occurs when black squares are bounded by open squares on too many sides and the solution path cannot accommodate all of them. For example, returning to the puzzle that was started in Figure 4.24, another possible clue might be placed in the sixth row, indicating two black squares to the left. Again, this looks like it might have potential (see Figure 4.27). However, when we start to drawn in the path piece that are determined by these new black squares, we find that the bottom left corner is completed nicely but that there is now an impossible situation on the left side of the grid (see Figure 4.28). The black square in the third column of the sixth row needs to have a path both above and to the left, and this leaves another path piece stranded on the left side of the grid. With practice, puzzle designers can learn to avoid these kinds of problems in creating new Yajilin puzzles.

Figure 4.25. First bad clue.

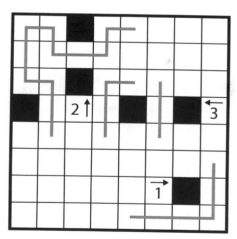

Figure 4.26. Odd numbers of endpoints.

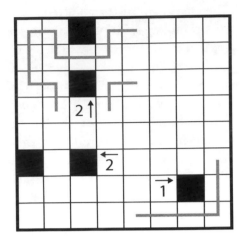

Figure 4.27. Second bad clue.

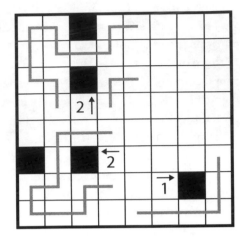

Figure 4.28. A stranded endpoint.

It is also important to remember that there are two types of boxes in the grid that are not part of the path—the black squares and the clue boxes that have an arrow and a number in them. Even though these two types of boxes are not part of the path, they behave differently and are used by a puzzle designer in different ways. A box with a black square is usually more useful in determining a path, because when one is placed, the adjacent squares must contain either a clue box or a part of the path. This often allows creators and solvers to place straight lines and Ls next to the black squares when they are bounded. However, as seen in the previous two examples, poor placement of black squares can lead to impossible situations, so puzzle designers must be careful not to place too many black squares or to put them in arrangements that cause problems.

Clue boxes with arrows and numbers in them may be less helpful for determining a path, because boxes that are adjacent to them could contain either part of the path or a black square. However, if a puzzle designer wants to create a puzzle with a theme, the clue boxes can be helpful in doing so. For example, a puzzle might begin with only one type of number (e.g., Figures 4.29 and 4.30), with arrows pointing in only one direction (e.g., Figures 4.31 and 4.32), or with clues placed in boxes that create a symmetrical design (e.g., Figures 4.33 and 4.34). These kinds of themes often provide an extra challenge to the puzzle designer and can be a lot of fun to create.

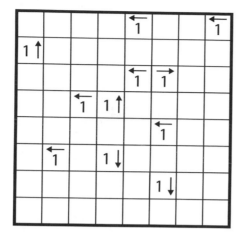

Figure 4.29. All ones.

Figure 4.30. All ones solution.

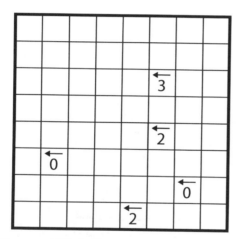

Figure 4.31. Left arrows.

Figure 4.32. Left arrows solution.

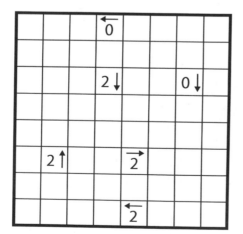

Figure 4.33. Rotational symmetry.

Figure 4.34. Rotational symmetry solution.

Yajilin Worksheets

On the next two pages are two examples of Yajilin puzzles and their solutions. Use these two examples to determine what you think the goal of a Yajilin puzzle is and what the rules are for determining the unique solution.

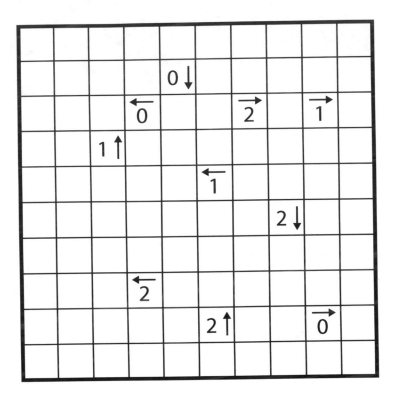

Spatial Reasoning Puzzles That Make Kids Think! © Prufrock Press Inc.

Yajilin Worksheets

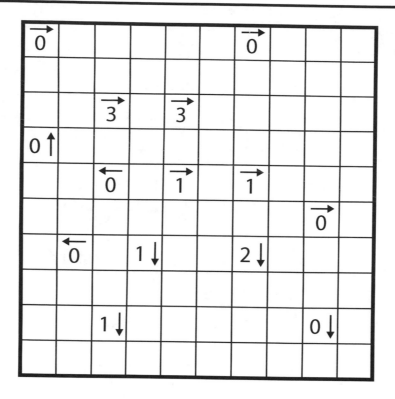

8 x 8 Yajilin Puzzles

1

2

3

Solutions on p. 138.

4

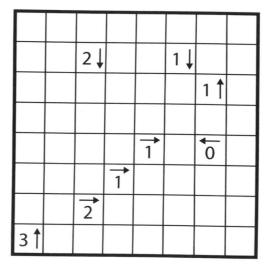

5

6

7

8

9

Solutions on p. 138.

10

11

12

Solutions on p. 138.

10 x 10 Yajilin Puzzles

1

2

Solutions on p. 139.

3

(10×10 grid puzzle with the following clue cells:)
- 1↓
- 4← (4 with left arrow)
- 1↑
- 2→
- 0→
- 2← (2 with left arrow)
- 4→
- 1↑

4

(10×10 grid puzzle with the following clue cells:)
- 1↑
- 1↓
- 1↓
- 2↓
- 1→
- 1↑
- 3→
- 1↑
- 1↓
- 1↑
- 1↑
- 2→
- 1↑
- 1← (1 with left arrow)
- 1→
- 1↑

Solutions on p. 139.

5

6

Solutions on p. 139.

Spatial Reasoning Puzzles That Make Kids Think! © Prufrock Press Inc.

7

8

Solutions on p. 140.

9

10

Solutions on p. 140.

Spatial Reasoning Puzzles That Make Kids Think! © Prufrock Press Inc.

11

```
      ┌───┬───┬───┬───┬───┬───┬───┬───┬───┬───┐
      │   │   │→3 │   │   │   │   │   │   │   │
      ├───┼───┼───┼───┼───┼───┼───┼───┼───┼───┤
      │   │   │   │   │   │   │   │   │   │   │
      ├───┼───┼───┼───┼───┼───┼───┼───┼───┼───┤
      │   │   │   │   │   │   │   │   │1↓ │   │
      ├───┼───┼───┼───┼───┼───┼───┼───┼───┼───┤
      │   │   │   │   │1↓ │   │   │   │   │   │
      ├───┼───┼───┼───┼───┼───┼───┼───┼───┼───┤
      │   │1↑ │   │   │   │   │   │   │   │   │
      ├───┼───┼───┼───┼───┼───┼───┼───┼───┼───┤
      │2↓ │   │   │   │   │   │→1 │   │   │   │
      ├───┼───┼───┼───┼───┼───┼───┼───┼───┼───┤
      │   │   │3↑ │   │   │   │   │   │0↓ │   │
      ├───┼───┼───┼───┼───┼───┼───┼───┼───┼───┤
      │   │1↑ │1↓ │   │   │   │←2 │   │   │   │
      ├───┼───┼───┼───┼───┼───┼───┼───┼───┼───┤
      │   │   │   │   │   │   │   │   │   │   │
      ├───┼───┼───┼───┼───┼───┼───┼───┼───┼───┤
      │   │   │   │   │   │   │   │   │   │   │
      └───┴───┴───┴───┴───┴───┴───┴───┴───┴───┘
```

12

```
      ┌───┬───┬───┬───┬───┬───┬───┬───┬───┬───┐
      │   │   │   │   │   │   │   │   │←1 │   │
      ├───┼───┼───┼───┼───┼───┼───┼───┼───┼───┤
      │   │   │   │   │   │   │   │   │   │   │
      ├───┼───┼───┼───┼───┼───┼───┼───┼───┼───┤
      │   │   │   │   │   │   │   │   │   │   │
      ├───┼───┼───┼───┼───┼───┼───┼───┼───┼───┤
      │   │   │   │3↑ │   │   │3↑ │   │   │   │
      ├───┼───┼───┼───┼───┼───┼───┼───┼───┼───┤
      │0↑ │1↓ │   │   │   │   │   │   │←2 │   │
      ├───┼───┼───┼───┼───┼───┼───┼───┼───┼───┤
      │   │   │   │   │   │   │   │   │   │   │
      ├───┼───┼───┼───┼───┼───┼───┼───┼───┼───┤
      │   │   │   │   │   │   │   │   │   │   │
      ├───┼───┼───┼───┼───┼───┼───┼───┼───┼───┤
      │   │   │   │   │   │   │←2 │   │   │   │
      └───┴───┴───┴───┴───┴───┴───┴───┴───┴───┘
```

Solutions on p. 140.

18 x 10 Yajilin Puzzles

1

2

Solutions on p. 141.

Spatial Reasoning Puzzles That Make Kids Think! © Prufrock Press Inc.

Name:______________________________ Date: ______________________

3

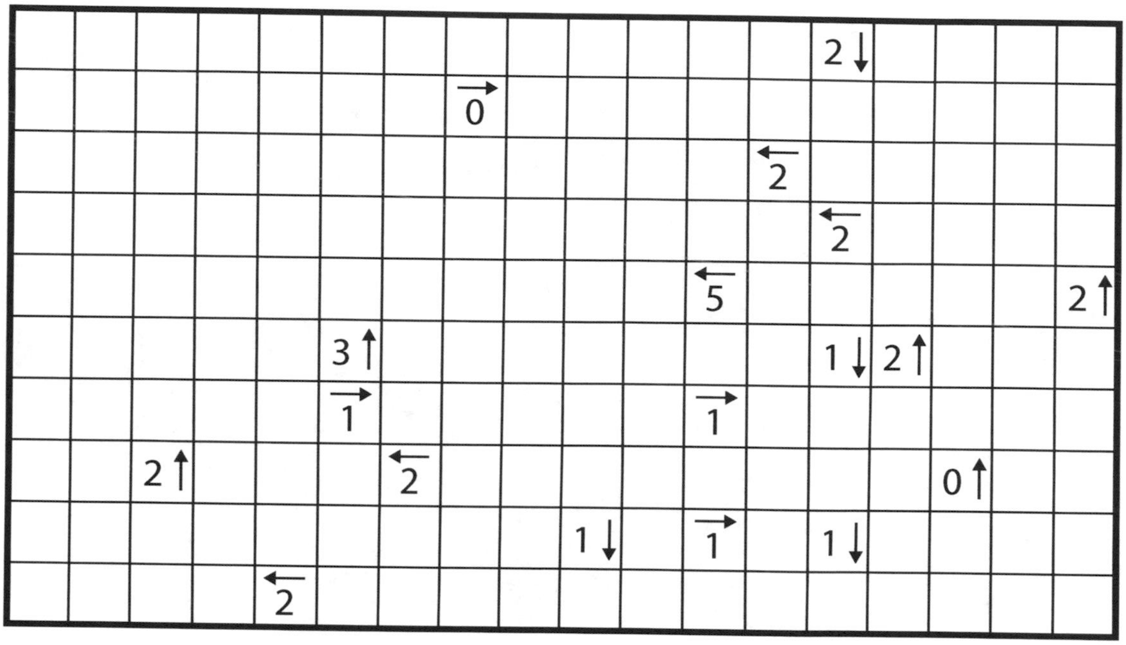

4

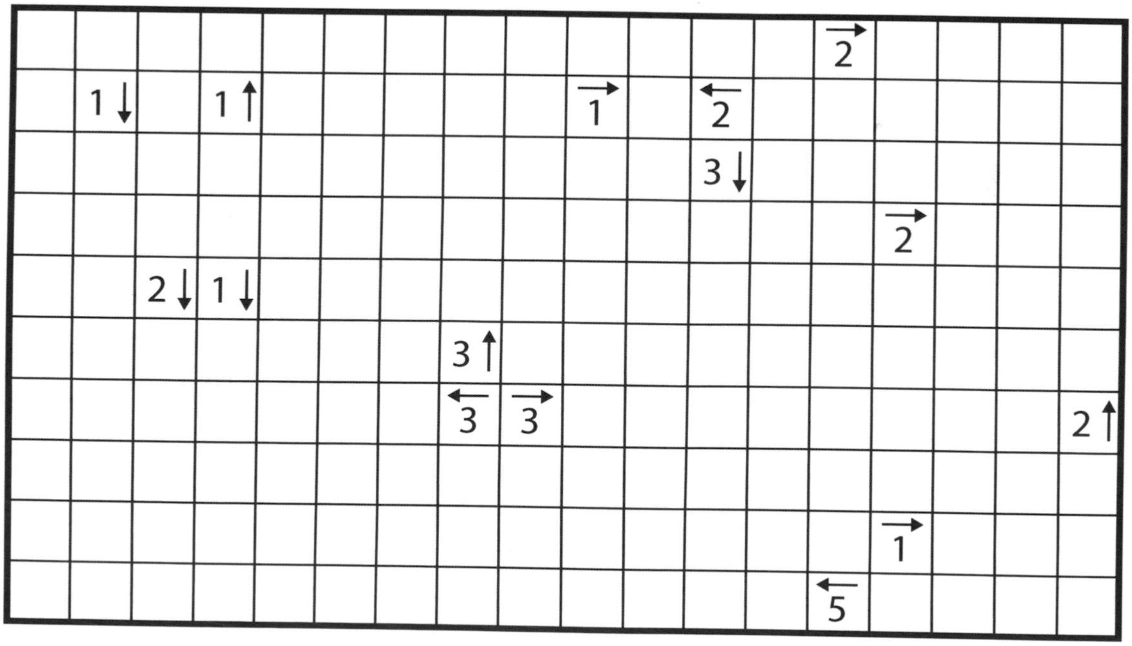

Solutions on p. 141 and p. 142

Name: _____ **Date:** _____

5

6

Solutions on p. 142.

Spatial Reasoning Puzzles That Make Kids Think! © Prufrock Press Inc.

Name:______________________ Date: ______________________

7

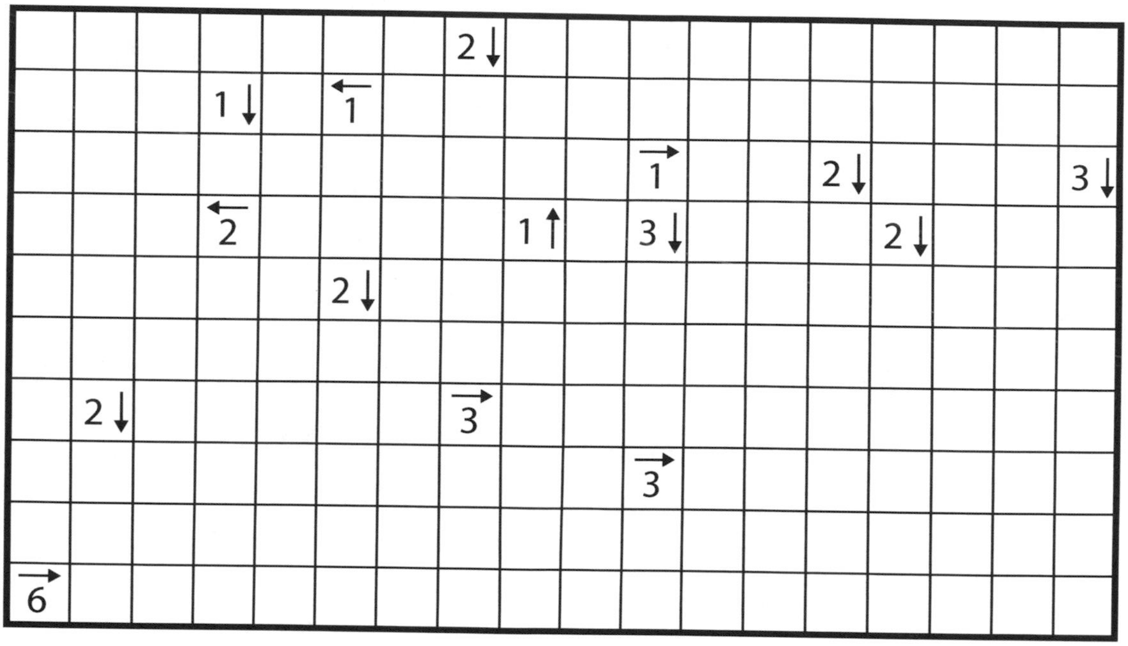

8

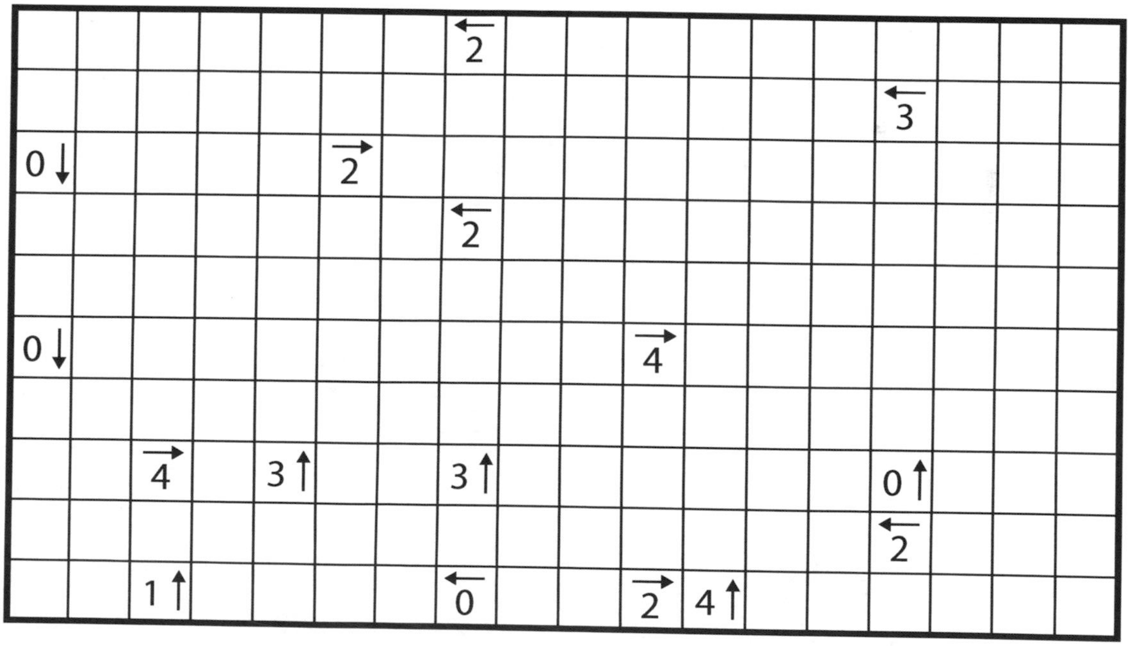

Solutions on p. 143.

9

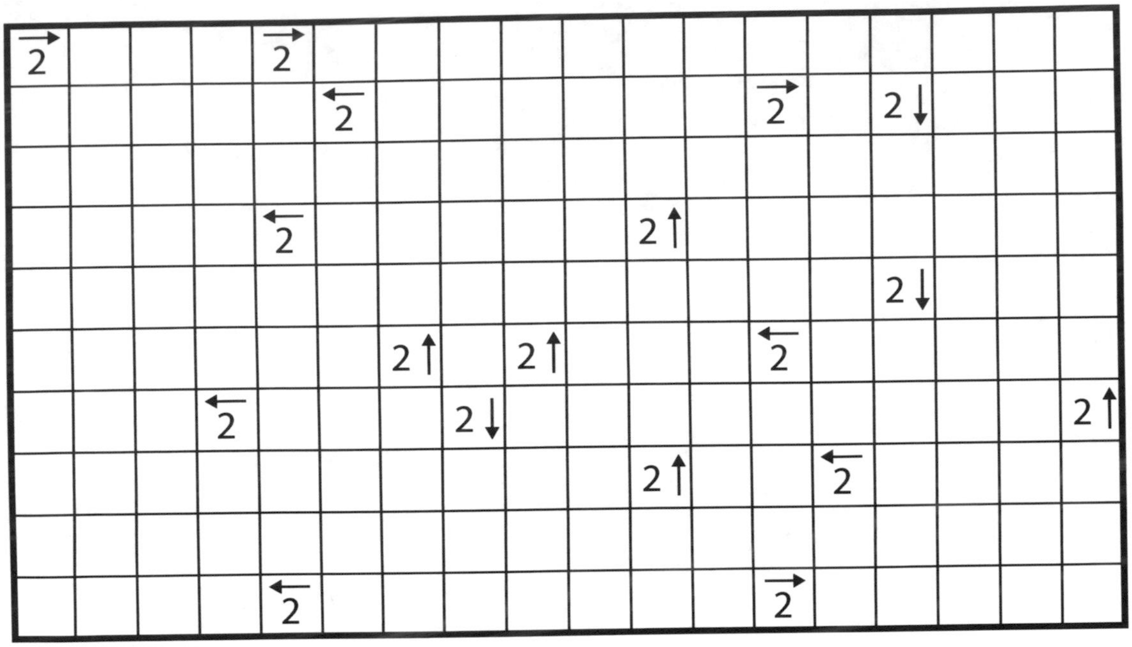

2→ ... 2→ ... 2← ... 2→ ... 2↓ ... 2← ... 2↑ ... 2↓ ... 2↑ ... 2↑ ... 2← ... 2↑ ... 2← ... 2↓ ... 2↑ ... 2← ... 2← ... 2→

10

2↓ ... 2← ... 1↑ ... 1↓ ... 1→ ... 0↑ ... 2↑ ... 1→ ... 2↑ ... 2← ... 2→ ... 1→ ... 3↑ ... 1↑ ... 0↓ ... 2↓ ... 1← ... 2← ... 3← ... 3← ... 1↑ ... 3↑ ... 2↑ ... 2→

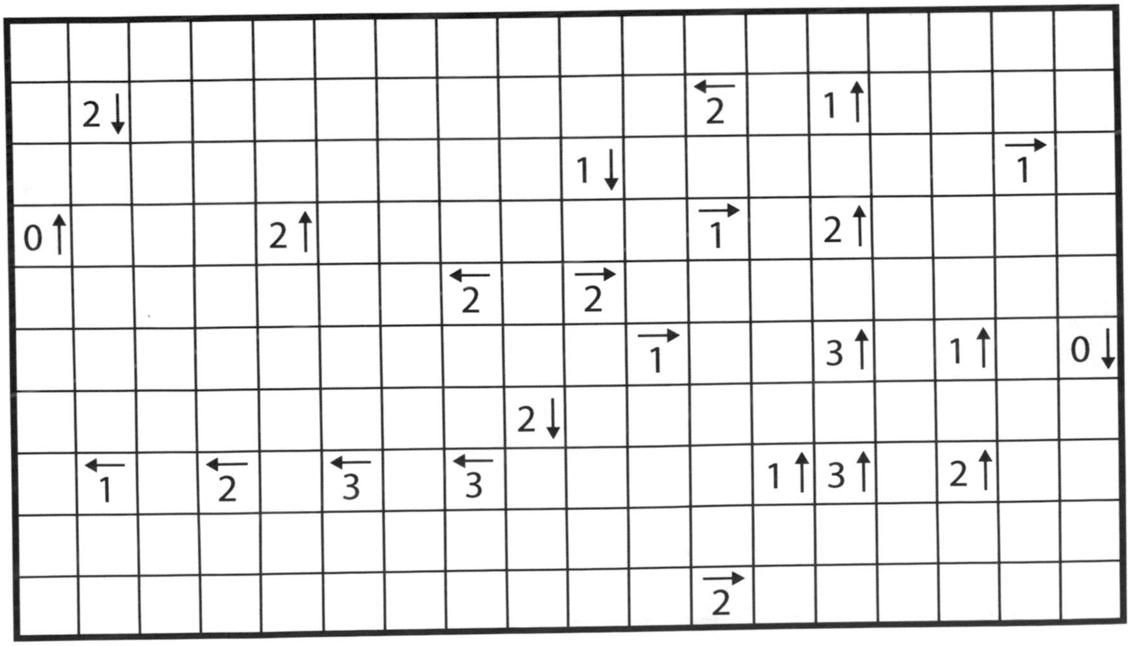

Solutions on p. 143 and p. 144.

Spatial Reasoning Puzzles That Make Kids Think! © Prufrock Press Inc.

11

12

Solutions on p. 144.

Blank Grids to Create Your Own Puzzles

The following pages have blank grids to allow you and your students to create original Slitherlink, Hashiwokakero, Masyu, and Yajilin puzzles. Enjoy!

6 x 6 Slitherlink Puzzle Grids

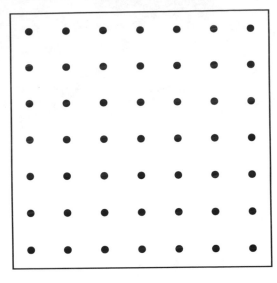

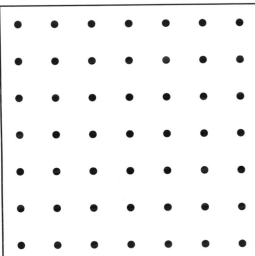

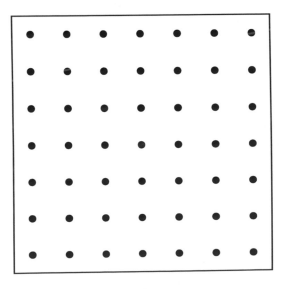

8 x 8 Slitherlink Puzzle Grids

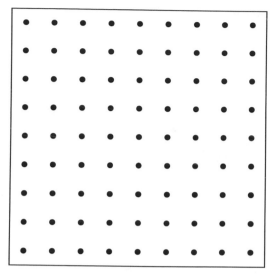

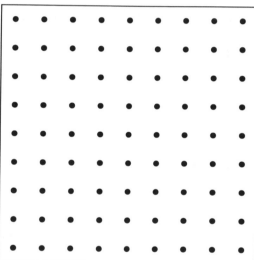

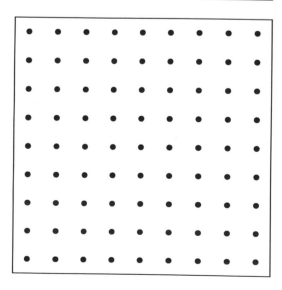

10 x 10 Slitherlink Puzzle Grids

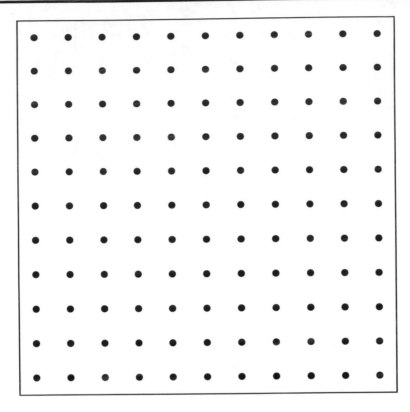

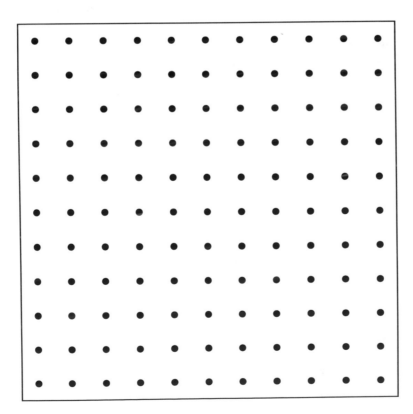

7 x 7 Hashiwokakero Puzzle Grids

Students should use the grids on this page to create their Hashiwokakero puzzles with their solutions. Then, they should overlay a copy of the blank frames on the next page and trace their circles and numbers onto the frames to create puzzles for others to solve.

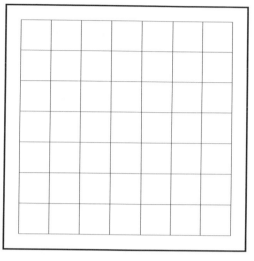

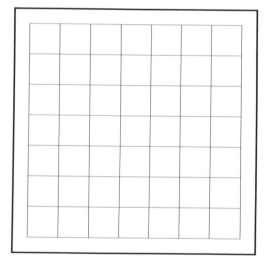

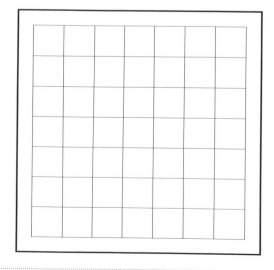

7 x 7 Hashiwokakero Blank Puzzle Grids

Spatial Reasoning Puzzles That Make Kids Think! © Prufrock Press Inc.

9 x 9 Hashiwokakero Puzzle Grids

Students should use the grids on this page to create their Hashiwokakero puzzles with their solutions. Then, they should overlay a copy of the blank frames on the next page and trace their circles and numbers onto the frames to create puzzles for others to solve.

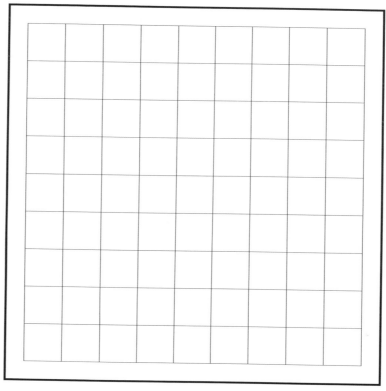

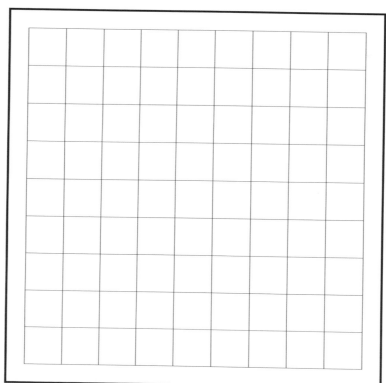

9 x 9 Hashiwokakero Blank Puzzle Grids

Spatial Reasoning Puzzles That Make Kids Think! © Prufrock Press Inc.

16 x 9 Hashiwokakero Puzzle Grids

Students should use the grids on this page to create their Hashiwokakero puzzles with their solutions. Then, they should overlay a copy of the blank frames on the next page and trace their circles and numbers onto the frames to create puzzles for others to solve.

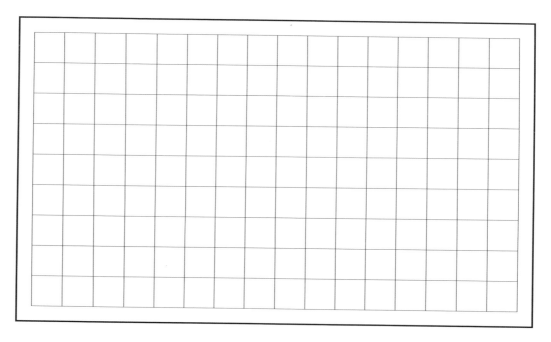

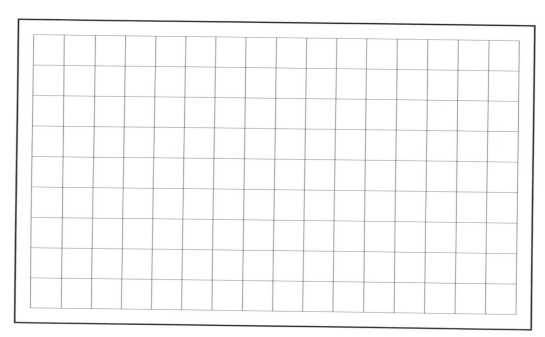

16 x 9 Hashiwokakero Blank Puzzle Grids

6 x 6 Masyu Puzzle Grids

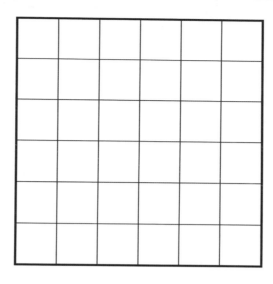

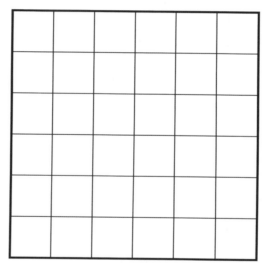

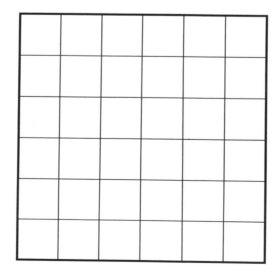

8 x 8 Masyu Puzzle Grids

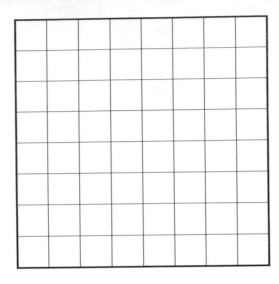

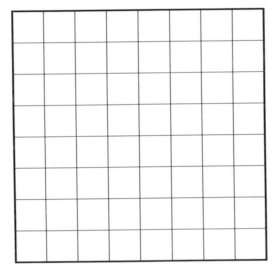

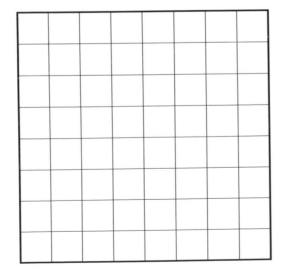

10 x 10 Masyu Puzzle Grids

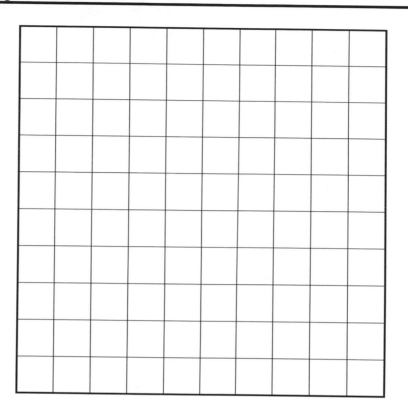

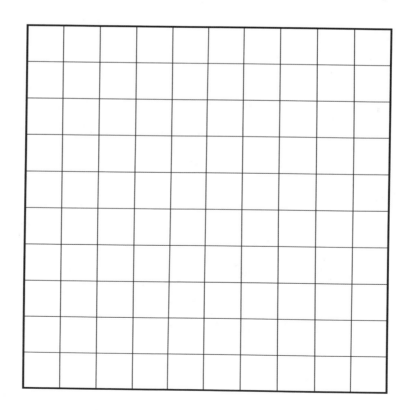

8 x 8 Yajilin Puzzle Grids

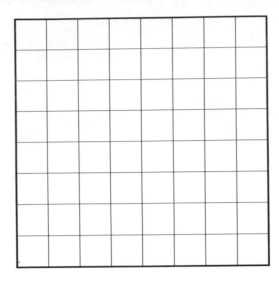

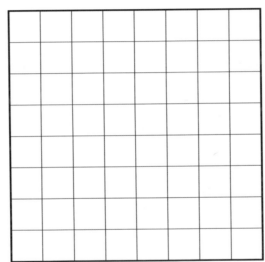

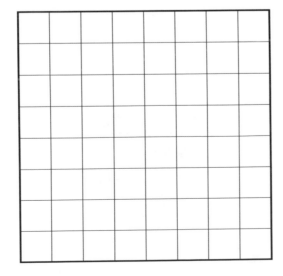

10 x 10 Yajilin Puzzle Grids

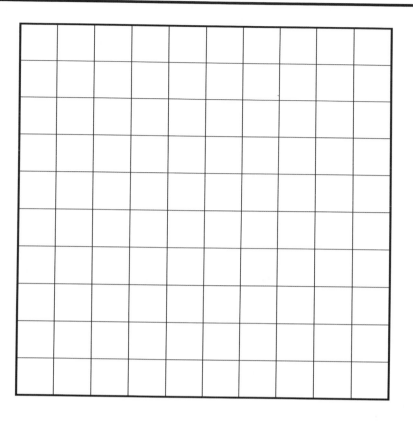

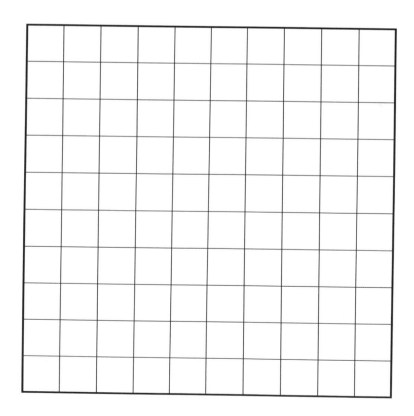

18 x 10 Yajilin Puzzle Grids

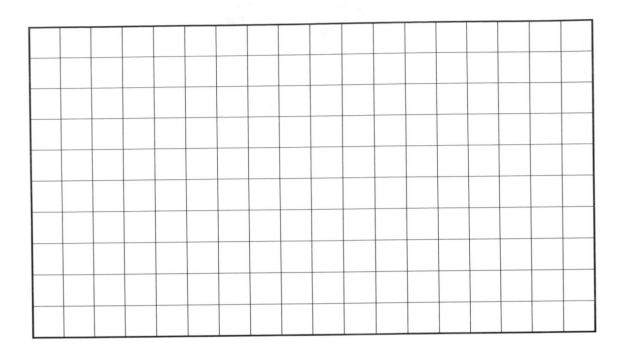

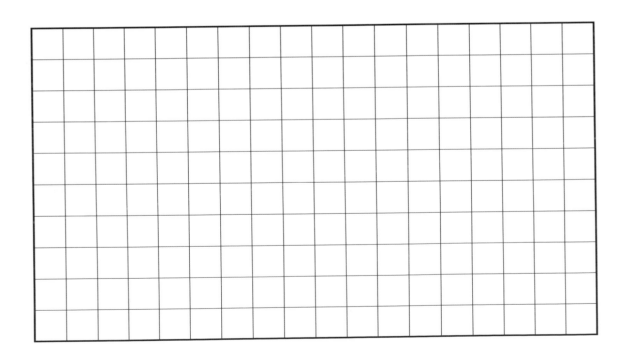

Solutions

6 x 6 Slitherlink Puzzles

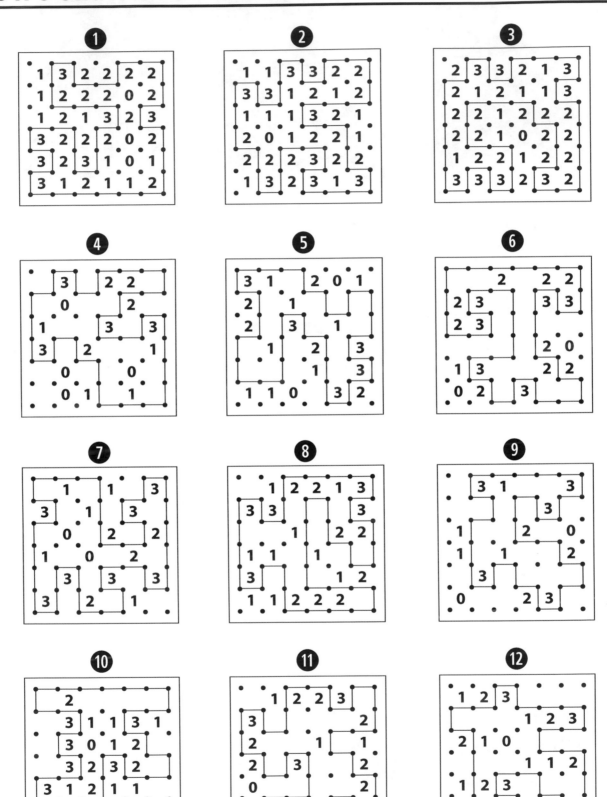

8 x 8 Slitherlink Puzzles

1

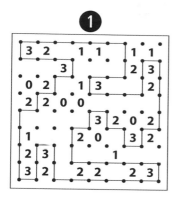

2

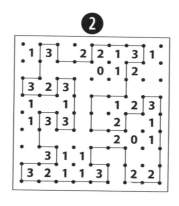

3

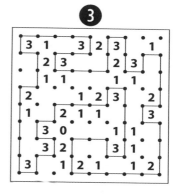

4

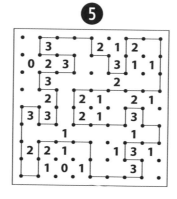

5

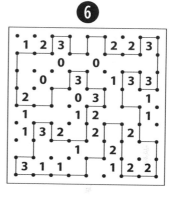

6

7

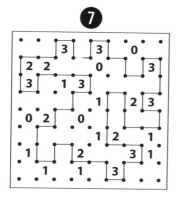

8

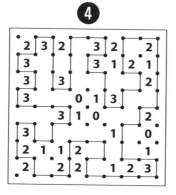

9

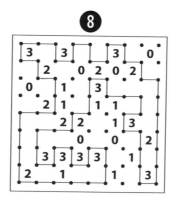

10

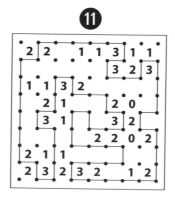

11

12

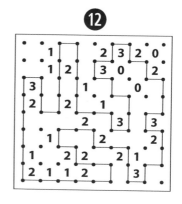

10 x 10 Slitherlink Puzzles

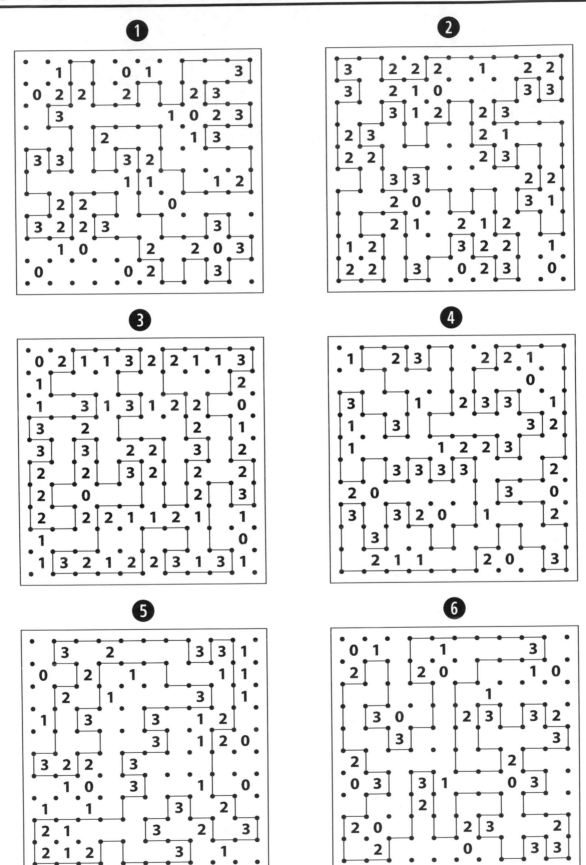

10 x 10 Slitherlink Puzzles

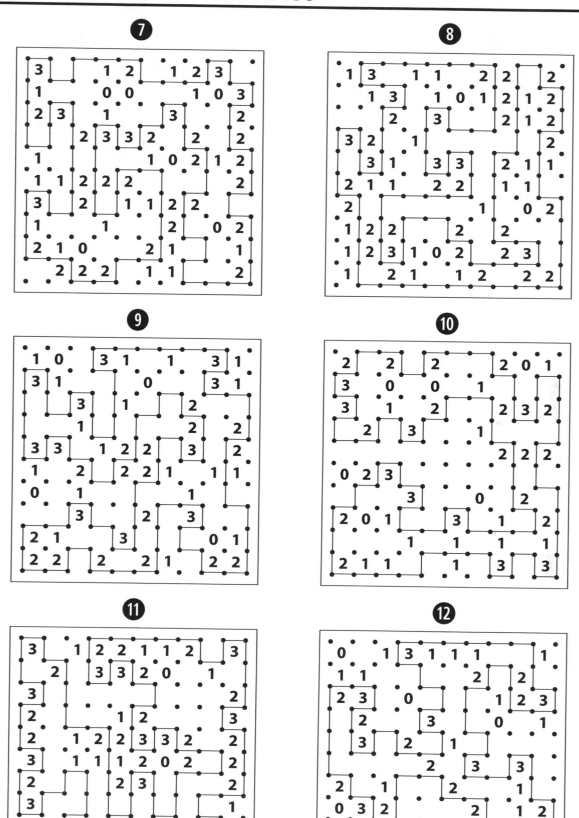

7 x 7 Hashiwokakero Puzzles

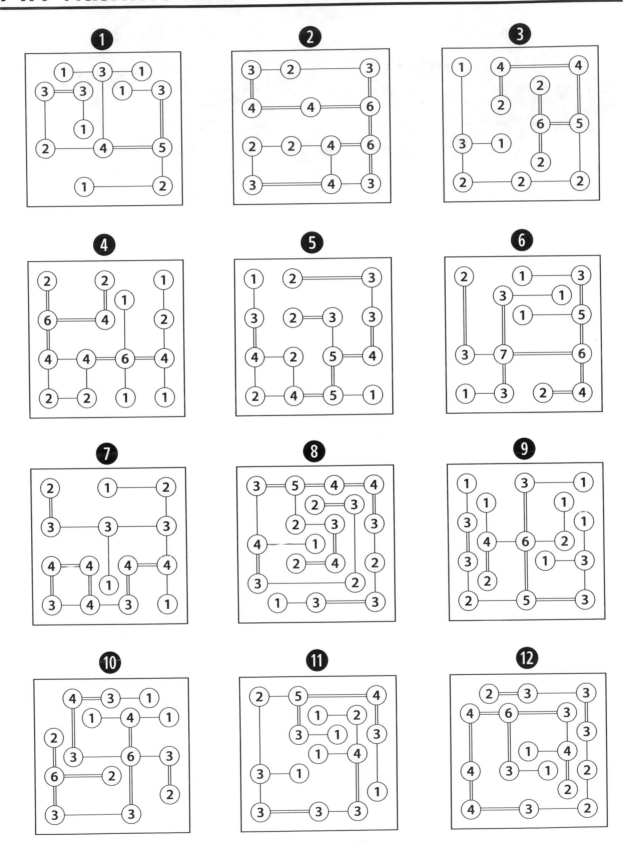

9 x 9 Hashiwokakero Puzzles

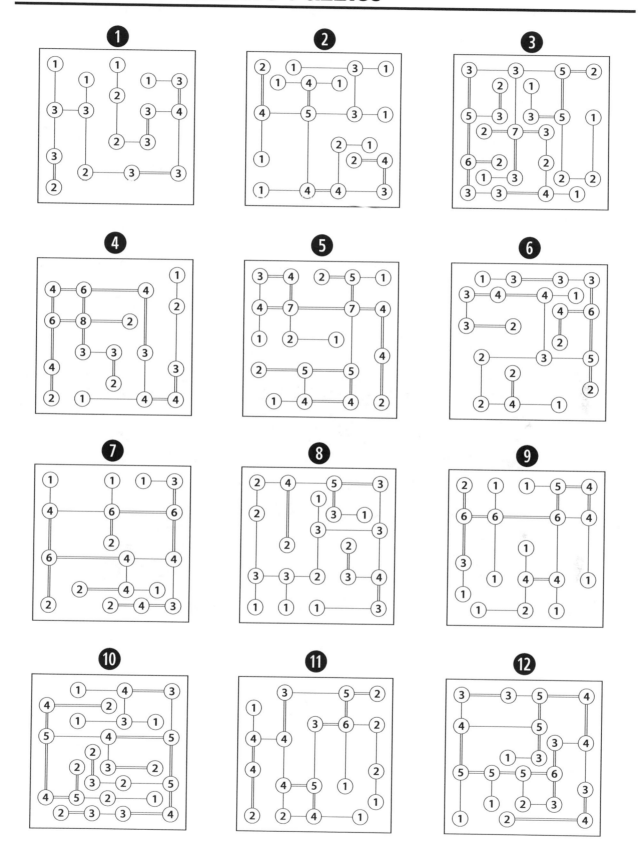

16 x 9 Hashiwokakero Puzzles

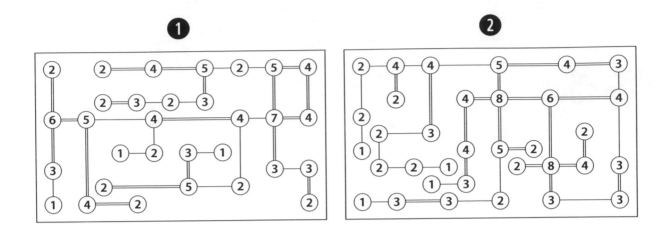

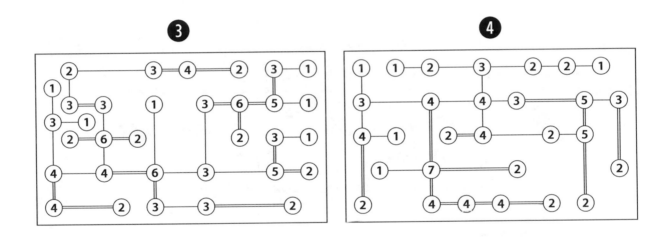

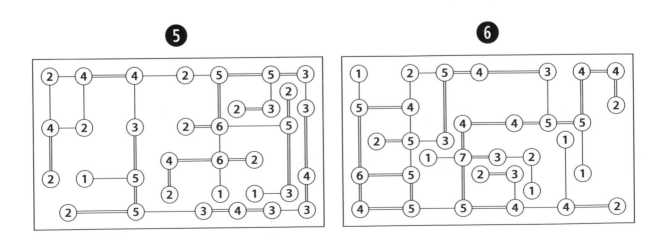

16 x 9 Hashiwokakero Puzzles

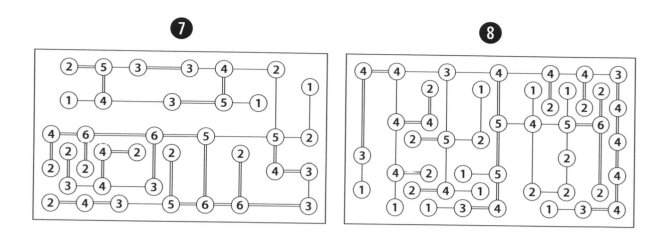

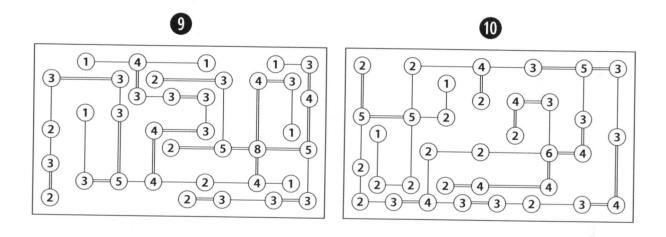

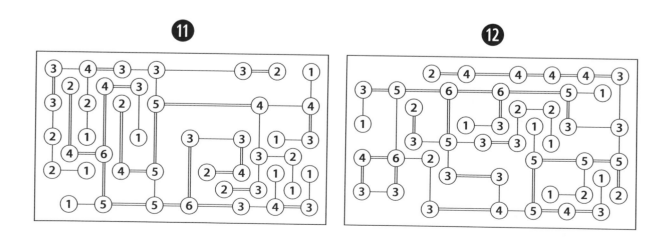

6 x 6 Masyu Puzzles

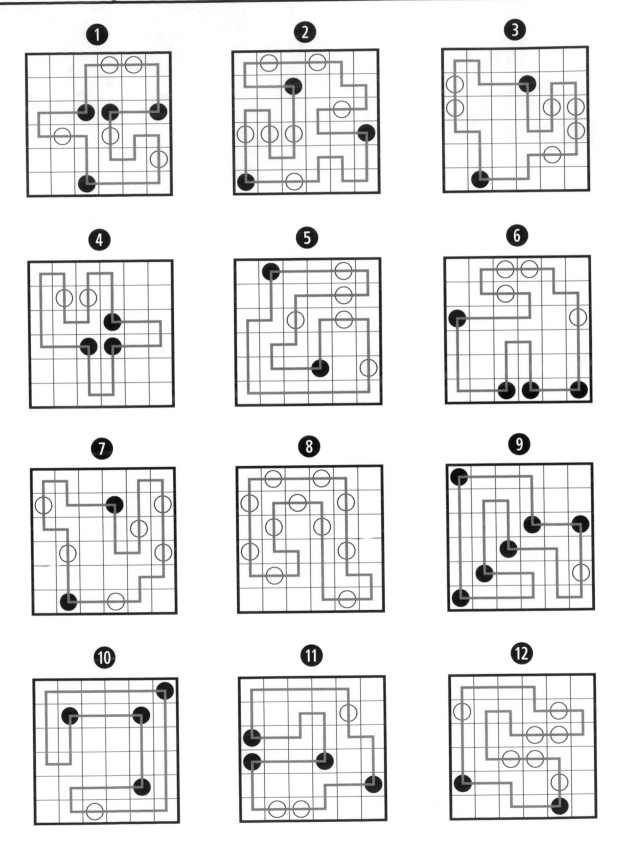

8 x 8 Masyu Puzzles

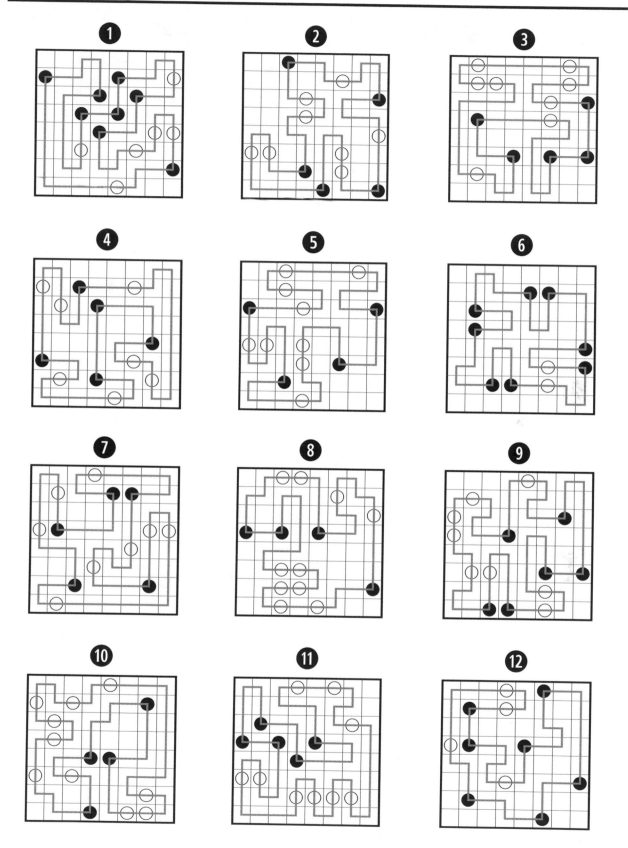

10 x 10 Masyu Puzzles

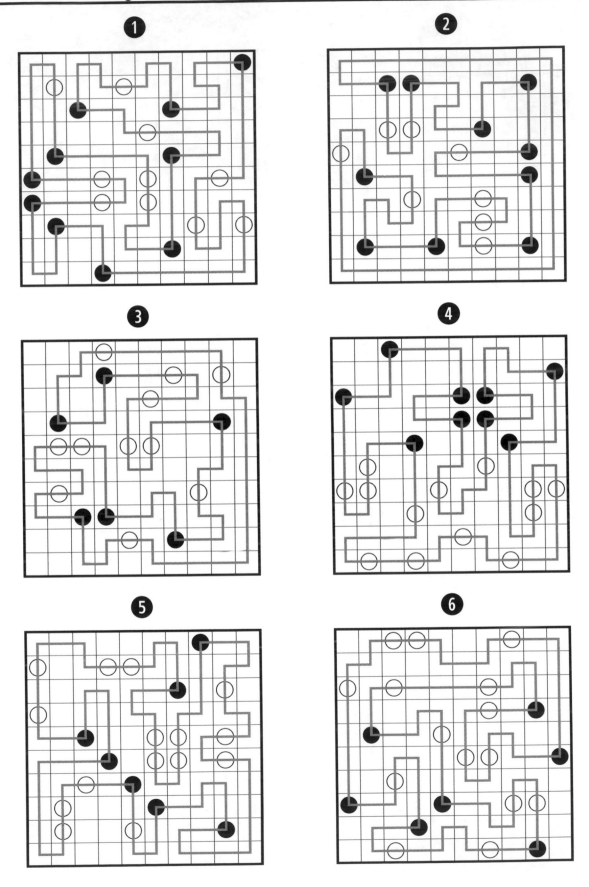

10 x 10 Masyu Puzzles

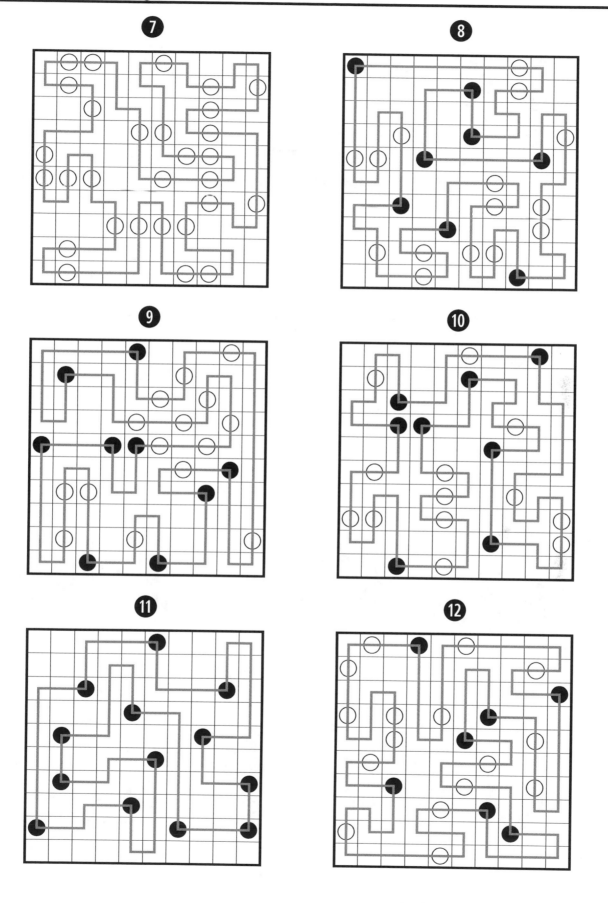

8 x 8 Yajilin Puzzles

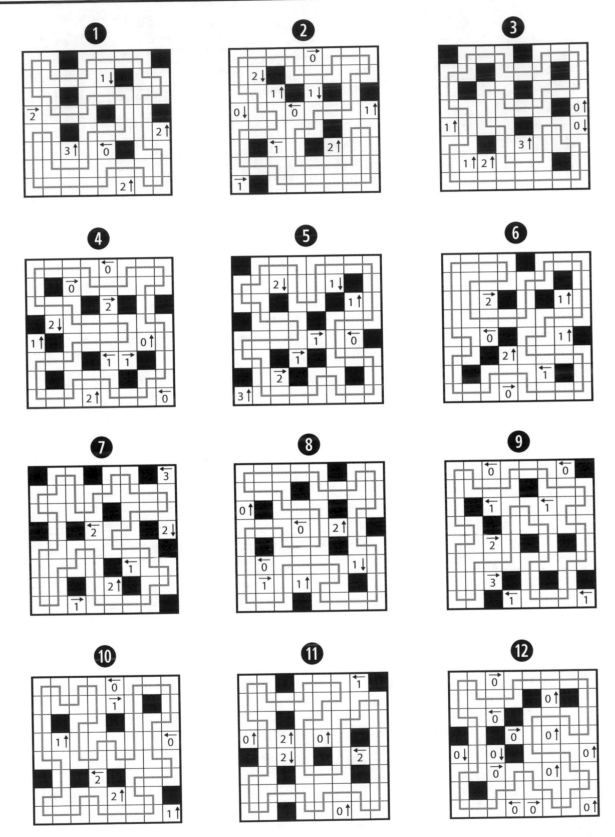

10 x 10 Yajilin Puzzles

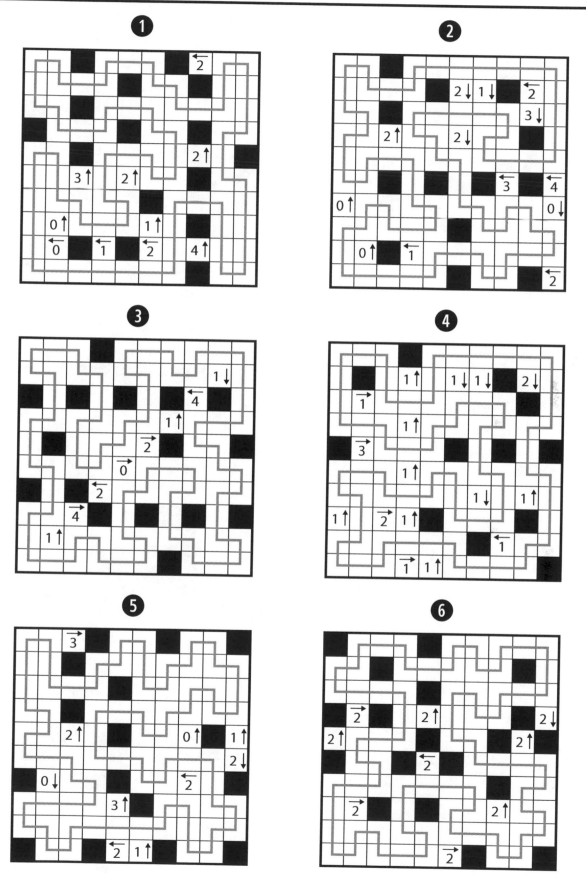

10 x 10 Yajilin Puzzles

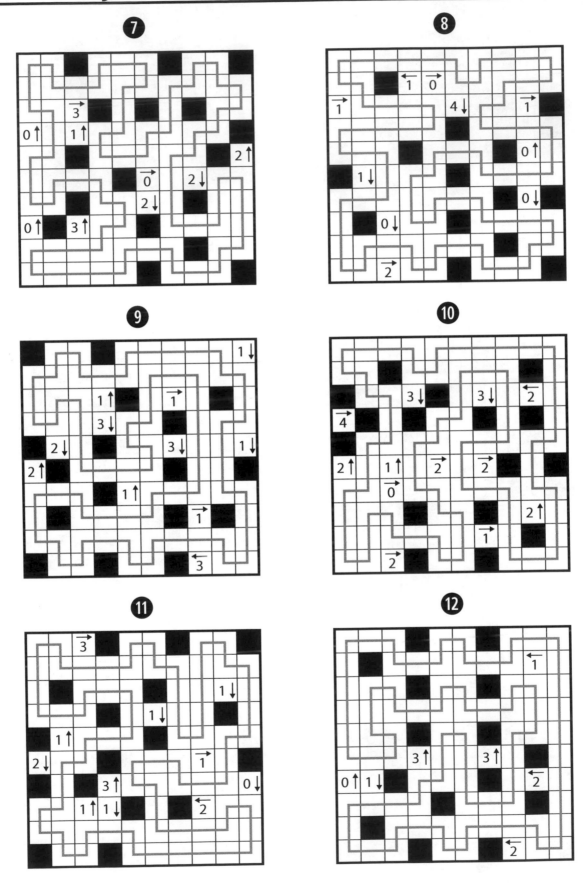

18 x 10 Yajilin Puzzles

1

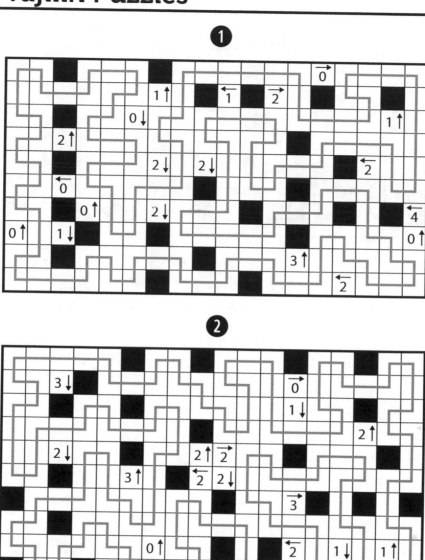

2

3

18 x 10 Yajilin Puzzles

4

5

6

18 x 10 Yajilin Puzzles

7

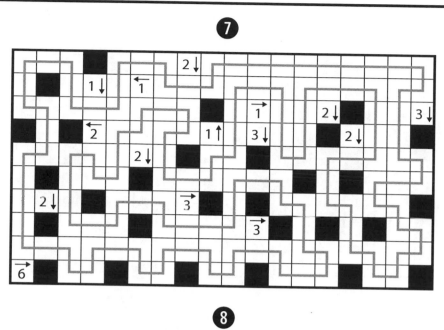

8

9

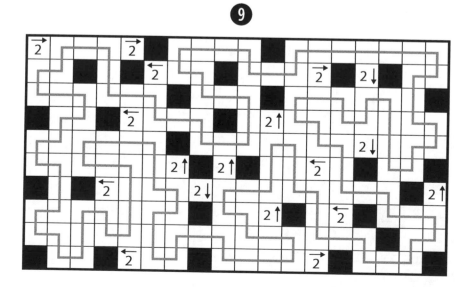

18 x 10 Yajilin Puzzles

10

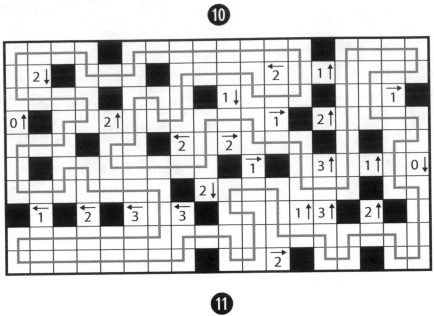

11

12

References

Ben-Chaim, D., Lappan, G., & Houang, R. T. (1988). The effect of instruction on spatial visualization skills of middle school boys and girls. *American Educational Research Journal, 25,* 51–71.

Battista, M. T. (1990). Spatial visualization and gender differences in high school geometry. *Journal for Research in Mathematics Education, 21,* 47–60.